Better Homes and Gardens®

Home Security

YOUR GUIDE TO PROTECTING YOUR FAMILY

Better Homes and Gardens® Books
Des Moines, Iowa

✓

Better Homes and Gardens® Books
An imprint of Meredith® Books

Home Security: Your Guide to Protecting Your Family
Editor: Paula Marshall
Writer: Jim Hufnagel
Technical Editor: Alan Keyes
Designer: David Jordan
Associate Art Director: Lynda Haupert
Copy Chief: Catherine Hamrick
Copy and Production Editor: Terri Fredrickson
Contributing Copy Editors: Carol Boker, Martin Miller
Contributing Proofreaders: Steve Hallam, Margaret Smith
Contributing Illustrators and Designers: The Art Factory
Electronic Production Coordinator: Paula Forest
Editorial and Art Assistants: Kaye Chabot, Mary Lee Gavin, Karen Schirm
Production Director: Douglas Johnston
Production Manager: Pam Kvitne
Assistant Prepress Manager: Marjorie J. Schenkelberg

Thanks to: Interactive Technologies, Inc. (ITI), North St. Paul, MN, photographs and illustrations (pgs. 47, 48, 49) used with permission; Digital Monitoring Products (DMP) Springfield, MO; photographs and illustrations (pgs. 42, 43, 45) used with permission.
Photographs: © John Glover, Farnham Surrey, England, shrubs on page 8; © PhotoDisc, Inc., pages 4 (bottom), 56, 58, 59, 61, 68-69, 70-71, 74, 76, 77, back cover.

Meredith® Books
Editor in Chief: James D. Blume
Design Director: Matt Strelecki
Managing Editor: Gregory H. Kayko
Executive Editor, Shelter Books: Denise L. Caringer

Director, Sales & Marketing, Retail: Michael A. Peterson
Director, Sales & Marketing, Special Markets: Rita McMullen
Director, Sales & Marketing, Home & Garden Center Channel: Ray Wolf
Director, Operations: George A. Susral
Vice President, General Manager: Jamie L. Martin

Better Homes and Gardens® Magazine
Editor in Chief: Jean LemMon
Executive Building Editor: Joan McCloskey

Meredith Publishing Group
President, Publishing Group: Christopher Little
Vice President, Consumer Marketing & Development: Hal Oringer

Meredith Corporation
Chairman and Chief Executive Officer: William T. Kerr
Chairman of the Executive Committee: E. T. Meredith III

All of us at Better Homes and Gardens® Books are dedicated to providing you with information and ideas you need to enhance your home. We welcome your comments and suggestions about this book on home security. Write to us at: Better Homes and Gardens® Books, Do-It-Yourself Editorial Department, LN116, 1716 Locust St., Des Moines, IA 50309–3023.

If you would like to purchase any of our books, check wherever quality books are sold.

Note to the Reader: Due to differing conditions, tools, and individual skills, Meredith Corporation assumes no responsibility for any damages, injuries suffered, or losses incurred as a result of following the information published in this book. Before beginning any project, review the instructions carefully, and if any doubts or questions remain, consult local experts or authorities. Because local codes and regulations vary greatly, always check with local authorities to ensure that your project complies with all applicable local codes and regulations. Always read and observe all of the safety precautions provided by any tool or equipment manufacturer, and follow all accepted safety procedures.

Contents

Section 1 HOME SECURITY BASICS 4

Protecting your family and possessions starts with the nuts-and-bolts basics. Here's what you need to know to choose and install the key components of home security. Plus, you'll find tips for improving the safety of your home.

Section 2 STRATEGIES FOR SAFETY AND SECURITY 56

Taking charge of personal security and safety also requires thinking about your options and evaluating your lifestyle. In this section, you'll learn the essential strategies for keeping your family and home safe and secure.

Home Security
Basics

Take a good look around your house: Does it invite or deter a would-be burglar?

Many of the best ways to improve the security of your home are surprisingly simple. Smart home maintenance, good lighting, and a few good locks go a long way in reducing your home's curb appeal to burglars.

When evaluating your home's security, start by considering two P's: Perimeter and Points of Entry. That's the way a prowler would view your home.

Perimeter applies to the yard and exterior night lighting. Trees and bushes planted close to the house and left untrimmed offer ready cover to an intruder. A yard without a fence makes sneaking in and out easier. A ladder or tools left on the lawn can be used to break in.

If these things make your home look inviting during the day, a prowler may come back at night to scope out the lighting. A house left in the dark all evening, inside or out, isn't going to shed any light on illegal activity and makes a burglar's entry and exit almost undetectable.

Points of entry are, of course, all your doors and windows—even windows above the first floor. If you leave any windows or doors open most of the time or if they are in obvious poor repair, a burglar can get in and out quickly. Start by evaluating exterior doors— nearly 90 percent of all illegal entries are right through a door.

For some more specific advice on evaluating the security of your home, take the quiz at right. It will give you an idea of what you need to do to improve your home's security. And, you'll want to consider how you live in your home. For example, if you have good locks but often don't bother to use them, getting better locks won't increase your security. Getting in the practice of locking the door will help.

Your family's lifestyle is especially important when evaluating electronic alarm systems. These systems have become fairly popular, and the options available are staggering. If you have a good idea of how your family will use the security system, you're more likely to get just what you need—not too much, not too little. And these systems work best in homes that have covered the security basics.

The goal is to feel safe and comfortable in and around your home. Keep that in mind as you evaluate your home and prioritize the list of security home improvement projects.

How Secure Is Your Home?

You want to improve your home's security, but you're not sure where to start. Evaluating it, inside and out, with this quiz will give you a good overall security picture, and the weakest spots will likely jump out at you.

You probably won't be surprised by the results. Some things you likely know need to be corrected, but they haven't been a priority to you. Replacing a door or lock isn't the most glamorous of home-improvement projects. Other things you may have allowed for the sake of convenience, such as a key stashed under the mat or "hidden" in the garage. Even a third-rate burglar who's mildly determined to get in your house will look for a key.

Be objective. You create a false sense of security when you downplay your home's current shortcomings—a door that wiggles in its frame, even if it's just a touch, is not secure. Conversely, there's no need to panic about shortcomings—adding a dead bolt is most likely sufficient to secure a solid door that's in a reinforced frame; rebuilding the door is going a tad overboard.

Location and Lifestyle

☐ Have there been four or more burglaries in your neighborhood in the last few years?
☐ Do you live a few blocks from a major highway or adjacent to a wooded area?
☐ Is your home unoccupied at regular times each day?
☐ Do have unusually valuable jewelry, artwork, collections, or electronic equipment in your home?
☐ Do you live on a cul-de-sac?
☐ Does your neighborhood lack a program for keeping an eye out for criminal activity?

An answer of *yes* to any of the above means you could have an above-average risk of a break-in—and now is the time to evaluate and improve the security of your home and neighborhood.

The House

☐ Do you keep a spare house key under a mat, in a flowerpot, or elsewhere outside?

☐ Do you have hollow-core doors leading into your house from the outside?
☐ Are any of your exterior doors *not* secured by a heavy-duty dead-bolt lock and reinforced strikeplate?
☐ Can your expensive stereo or computer system be easily seen by looking in a window?
☐ Is your pet door large enough to allow a person to squeeze through?

All of these make your house a more attractive target to burglars. And, all of them are relatively easy to fix. Now is the time to focus on these shortcomings and correct them.

The Yard

☐ Could a tree limb give an agile climber access to a second-story window or balcony?
☐ Do overgrown trees or shrubs prevent any of your doors or windows from being seen from the street or from a neighbor's house?
☐ Are all sides of your house well-lighted at night or equipped with motion-sensitive lights?
☐ Is your lawn well maintained, or does it look like your home may be unoccupied?
☐ Do you leave valuable lawn and garden equipment in your yard?

Home security is more than locks and solid doors. If a burglar can get close to your house without being detected, he has more time to get inside without being noticed. Your yard says a lot to a burglar casing homes in your neighborhood. Make sure your home tells the intruder to get lost!

When No One Is Home

☐ Do you use timers on some lights?
☐ Do you leave any doors or windows unlocked?
☐ Is your mail and newspaper picked up every day by a friend or neighbor?

When you're on vacation, your house should look as though you're still home. In this book, you'll find tips for making your home look lived in when you're not there.

Securing the **Outside**

Effective home security starts at the street; that's where burglars often begin "casing" a house.

The appearance of your home from the street can either invite intruders or send them looking for easier pickings. Head to the curb for a burglar's-eye view of your home.

Start by assessing the landscaping around your home. Overgrown or badly placed shrubs provide cover, and they obscure your view of approaches to the house. Tree branches near the house can provide a ladder of opportunity to upper-level windows or a skylight. Even an unruly lawn, which gives a nobody's-home look, can draw a thief's attention.

How easy is it to get to windows and doors? A burglar will assess how quickly and quietly he can get in and out of a home. An unfenced backyard that opens on an alley or an attached garage that doesn't have windows visible from the street or a neighbor's house can make for undetected access and exit.

How a house is lit, inside and out, sends a signal, too. For more about lighting, turn to page 10.

▶ *Security-smart landscaping needn't be boring. The low shrubs beside the walkway, border plantings along the porch, and hanging ferns placed high in front of the windows emphasize the charm of this cottage without obstructing the view from the street.*

Fortunately, many of the solutions that can make your house safer are simple. Start making your house less appealing to burglars by following these landscaping tips:

☐ **Pick up** the yard and driveway regularly. Old papers piling up by the front door are a signal that the home's empty or that nobody uses the front door. Ladders, picnic tables, and lawn chairs can become steps to reach windows; store them out of sight when not in use.

☐ **Saw off** branches close to the house or those that hang over the roof. And, on taller trees near the house, remove all limbs less than 7 feet from the ground to prevent anyone from climbing them to access the second floor.

☐ **Cut back** or remove tall shrubs near doors and walkways. The same goes for plantings that block the view to your windows, especially basement windows. Keep plantings trimmed to a height of 3 feet or shorter.

☐ **Use gravel** or pebbles under windows, and around sheds; it's noisy underfoot. And, plant low-growing thorny bushes.

☐ **Clear the view** to your neighbors' homes by trimming back bushes and trees. While you may enjoy your privacy, allowing your neighbors a clear view of the exterior of your house, especially its doors and windows, is a smart security choice.

Securing Your Yard
With a Fence

Thieves don't like fences because these structures make it difficult to enter a property, and even harder to haul stuff away. If you decide to fence your yard, you'll have several decisions to make:

☐ **Height.** Choose a fence tall enough to impede anyone trying to get into your yard; a minimum of 40 inches is recommended.

☐ **Style.** Look for a style solid enough to be a deterrent but open enough to allow visibility. Tall privacy fences, for example, can actually be inviting to an intruder: Once scaled, the fence provides excellent cover.

☐ **Legal requirements.** City codes and, where applicable, association covenants often dictate height, style, and placement of fences. Make sure your fence meets the requirements. And, have your lot surveyed before the fence is installed to be sure it's installed within your property lines.

Chain link (see page 9) is a popular choice because it's reasonably priced, can last a lifetime, and requires little or no maintenance. Some homeowners find the look of chain link too harsh, but there are options for improving its appearance. Black- or green-painted chain link blends surprisingly well into the landscape. Wood and plastic slats threaded through the links offer privacy and a windscreen. Airy vines growing up the fence greatly soften the appearance.

Homegrown Protection

Thorny hedges, dense shrubbery, and even rose bushes planted along the property line can create a barrier that most intruders won't want to cross. Just remember to keep your plantings trimmed for a clear view from the street or neighboring yards. The specific plantings that will work best for you depend on the growing conditions in your area, but here's a sampling of popular prickly plants:

☐ **Barberry.** A large group of dense, spiny shrubs used widely for hedge plantings, most barberries have small, bright yellow flowers, either single or in clusters and borne in great profusion. Many are decorative all winter. Deciduous barberries have deep red fall color.

Barberry

☐ **Hawthorn.** Tough, thorny hawthorn has delicate clusters of white or pink flowers in spring, glossy green foliage, orange to red fall color, and scarlet or yellow fruits.

Rose Shrub

☐ **Rose shrub.** Tough but beautiful, roses are an elegant way to deter prowlers. Roses, however, can be fussy plants. Talk to the staff at your local gardening center to find the hardiest varieties for your area.

Four-Legged Security

Many homeowners decide to install a fence after they've brought home a domestic canine security and affection unit—a family dog. Because dogs instinctively protect home and family—their hearing is keen, they're always on alert, and they make noise—they do deter some burglers. But they are not a complete solution. For example, if the dog is boarded when you vacation, your house is left unprotected. And not every dog is the perfect protector, however; there are a lot of variables in choosing the right dog for your family. Talk to a veterinarian or a trainer at an accredited dog-training school to help you find the right dog. Whatever breed you choose, the key to making a dog a great pet and home protector is training: You need to let the dog know what you want him to do—and what you don't want him to do. That's a lot more work than, say, plugging in a timer for security, but timers don't jump for joy when they see you pull in the driveway.

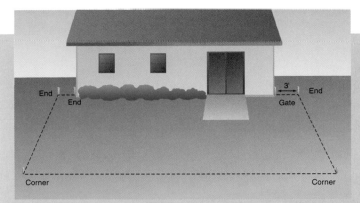

Installing a chain link fence

If you're considering installing a chain link fence, here's an overview of the process.

1 Mark locations of terminal posts—ends, corners, and gates. Three feet between gate posts (inside-to-inside) is the standard.

2 Dig holes and set terminal posts in concrete. Stretch a string tightly between terminal posts to help keep the rest of the posts in line, and at the right height. You can set them in concrete, too, for more stability. After all the posts are set, allow a day for the concrete to cure.

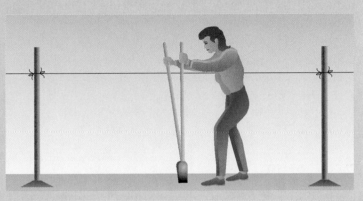

3 Install tension bands, post caps, and rail-end fittings on the terminal posts. Place a loop cap on each line post. Then insert the top rail through loop caps and into one rail-end fitting. Loosen the other end fitting, insert the rail, and reinstall.

Post cap

Loop cap

Rail-end fitting

Terminal post

Line post

Tension bar

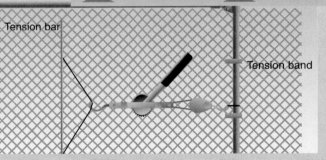

Tension bar

Tension band

4 Unroll the fencing on the ground on the outside of the posts. Slide a tension bar through the links at one end of the fencing. Lift the fencing and attach the bar to the tension bands. Lift and tie fencing loosely to the top rail with wire ties.

5 Thread a tension bar through fencing 4 feet from the terminal post at the opposite end, and stretch the fence taut with a fence stretcher. Pull up slack at the end and untie the fence just short of the terminal post. Slide a third tension bar through the fence at this end.

6 Attach the bar to tension bands and remove the stretcher. Secure fencing to the top rail and line posts with wire ties.

◄ This showcase house indicates how an effective lighting plan enhances a home and makes it safe—without glaring light or stark fixtures. The lighting would make a prowler feel very uncomfortable approaching the house, but friends and family can walk in and around it safely.

Security Lighting

Plenty of light, inside and out, is an excellent deterrent.

A well-lit interior at night tells would-be intruders it's likely someone is home, and exterior lighting exposes them if they approach a house. So, not surprisingly, burglars don't like light. Evaluate and improve the lighting around your house—both inside and out—to discourage prowlers and to increase safety.

Exterior Lighting

Select and place fixtures to provide an even blanket of light at entrances and to eliminate dark zones around the house where a person can hide. Brighter isn't necessarily better. Left on all night, glaring lights can annoy neighbors, blind visitors, and consume a great deal of electricity. Along walkways and in the landscaping, the artificial equivalent of a bright full moon (40-60 watts) is sufficient to discourage a burglar. For increased safety at entries, however, and for any security lights that you don't burn all night, use higher wattage fixtures. Follow these guidelines for lighting key areas:

☐ **At entry doors.** Use fixtures with two bulbs or pairs of one-bulb fixtures at each of your home's exterior doors, including doors you don't often use. A second bulb provides a greater spread of light, and ensures that the door won't be in the dark when one bulb burns out.

☐ **At the garage door.** Equipped with a motion detector, a fixture mounted above the garage door will turn on automatically every time someone—family, guests, or an unwanted visitor—enters your drive. Again, a double fixture provides both a back-up and increased lighting coverage.

☐ **Along walkways and driveways.** The path from the sidewalk or street to your house, and

Security
Lighting

from a detached garage to the house should be well-lit. A post light at the end of the driveway or a short walkway will do the job. For longer paths, use low-voltage fixtures to light the way.

☐ **Under eaves.** Use floodlights pointed downward from the eaves to wash the side of the house with light, and install them at corners to illuminate two sides of the house. Don't point lights away from the house; that leaves an unlit gap between house and light. And, where possible, place fixtures high enough to be unreachable by someone standing on the ground.

Choose a model with a motion sensor. The lights will come on only when someone or something comes into range. Or, if you want them on all night, choose a model with a photo-electric cell; the lights will turn on at dusk and off at dawn.

☐ **Under windows.** Mount fixtures on the ground, directing light up through trees and shrubs, to illuminate windows. Use low-wattage lights so you can still see out.

☐ **Under the deck.** A walkout basement or egress window that opens onto an area under a deck needs security lighting. For a door, a standard fixture with a motion sensor is a good choice. For a window, a low-voltage well light will provide gentle illumination.

Entry door lights

Path lighting

Under-eaves floodlights

Low-Voltage Lighting Solutions

Enhance both landscaping and security lighting with a low-voltage lighting system. You can usually install one of these inexpensive systems in an afternoon using only a screwdriver, a drill, and a garden spade. The heart of a low-voltage system is a weatherproof transformer that reduces the output to just 12 volts. This means you can't get shocked, even if you touch a bare wire or cut a cable with a garden tool. And, you don't need to worry about children playing near the lights or pets zapping themselves.

For even more security, economy, and convenience, use a specialized transformer. Options include a timer to automatically turn lights on and off, photo cells that turn the lights on at dusk and off at sunrise, or a photo cell/interval timer that turns lights on at dusk and off after an interval of your choice.

Mushroom lights

☐ **Mushroom lights** have large shades that direct light downward on walks, steps, or plants. Different shades and heights alter the width and intensity of the light.

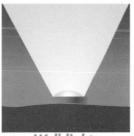

Floodlights

☐ **Floodlights** provide dramatic silhouettes, as well as excellent security. Mount them on walls or in trees. Or, for emphasis, install floodlights in the ground and point them skyward.

Well lights

☐ **Well lights** achieve dramatic uplighting effects on trees, shrubbery foliage, architectural features, or statuary.

☐ **Deck lights** along the railings add security by increasing the illuminated area around the house. They also improve safety when used to light steps to the yard.

Deck lights

Outdoor Grounded Timers

To control outdoor lighting, choose a grounded timer. To prevent anyone but you from changing the settings, be sure to place the timer inside a locked area, or choose a model with a locking cover.

Security Lighting

Interior Lighting

A house sitting dark all evening tells a prowler that no one is home. So does a light burning in the living room window all day. Timers are an inexpensive and effective way to solve the problem—and not just when your family is on vacation.

□ **Program a light** in the main living area to come on at nightfall and shut off at bedtime for overall safety and security. And, program a key outdoor light to come on at dusk. That way, no one ever comes home to a dark house.

□ **Think strategically** when setting timers for vacation. A single living room lamp that comes on at dusk and goes off at dawn every day won't fool someone who's watching the house.

Set lights to go on and off in different rooms at different times throughout the evening. If you have a multi-day timer, set it so your lights come on at different times each night. (This is also a good idea if you're often away from home in the evening.)

Some timers allow for randomized settings: The light comes on, for example, at 7:00 one evening, 7:20 the next, and 7:12 on the third night. Anyone watching the house will see a varied pattern and not the consistent pattern which hints that your home's unoccupied.

The lighting plan in the shaded box on page 15 lets you know what to consider in selecting and using sensors and timers.

□ **Assess interior** lighting from the exterior of your house. Turn the lights on, and then go outside to see what effect the lighting creates. For example, a row of blazing track lights near an uncurtained window can emphasize the emptiness of the house.

Sensors

The ultimate convenience is to have something turn lights on and off in response to specialized conditions. For these lights, sensors work best.

□ **Screw-in photoelectric sensors.** Installed in a lamp, photo sensors turn lights on at dusk, off at dawn. Use an indoor/outdoor model in a post light

to illuminate a walkway or driveway all night.

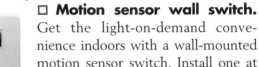

□ **Plug-in photo sensor.** Plug a lamp into this type of sensor for all-night lighting indoors—a good choice for an enclosed porch.

□ **Motion sensor wall switch.** Get the light-on-demand convenience indoors with a wall-mounted motion sensor switch. Install one at the head of the stairs or just inside the entrance from the garage or driveway. The light will stay on as long as someone is in the room or if you flip the switch.

□ **Motion sensor with floodlights.** Mounted under eaves, in front of the garage, or by a door, a motion sensor trips a light only when

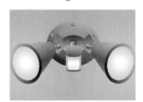

something comes within its range, then turns off after a preset amount of time. Many models have an override switch so you can turn the lights on manually, too. This is a good choice for any outdoor location.

Timers

You'll find timers galore at your local hardware store or home center. To give you an idea of the range of features, here are a few examples:

□ **Standard plug-in timer.** This type allows you to set just one or two on and off times per day. They are inexpensive and easy to program. Look for models that randomize daily on-off times by a few minutes. Use for living room and bedroom lamps.

☐ **Heavy-duty timer.** If you need more on-off options, and/or controls for electronic equipment (radio or TV) or appliances, choose a heavy-duty timer. With a digital model, times are set to the minute. Some allow for a slight randomization and some models have a battery backup so if the electricity goes out, the settings are kept.

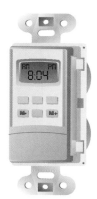

☐ **Wall-switch timer.** Use a wall-switch timer to control exterior door and other outdoor lights. For added convenience, choose a model with battery backup and manual override features.

A Lighting Plan

To ensure your home is lit for security, make two plans for each room—one plan for when you're home and another for when you're away. You can avoid scrambling to find timers by installing plug-in timers, program them for your vacation lighting plan but set them to "manual." That way, when you're getting ready for vacation, they're already in place. Flip the switch, and leave. For safety and security, leave main exterior lights on timers all the time. Here's a sample lighting plan, including times for vacation settings:

Interior Timers

☐ First floor:
Living room—light on 5-10:30 p.m.
Kitchen—light on 5-7 p.m., radio or television on for two hours in the evening.
☐ Second floor:
Bedroom—light on 7-7:30 p.m., again 9-11p.m.
Bathroom—light on 10-10:30 p.m., and once again sometime during the night.
☐ Basement: on for half an hour at different times each night.

Interior Sensors

☐ Basement entrance—light activated by motion sensor at top of stairs.
☐ Garage entry to the house—light activated by motion sensor.
☐ Living room—light activated by motion sensor when the timer isn't on.

Exterior Timers

☐ Front door: light on at dusk, off at midnight. (If the front of your house is not illuminated by a streetlight, leave this light on all night or install a photoelectric cell.)
☐ Post light: on at dusk, off at bedtime (or install a photoelectric cell).
☐ Backyard: low-voltage lights on at dusk, off at 10:30 p.m.

Exterior Sensors

☐ Back door, front of garage, shed doors, and under corner eaves: install photoelectric sensors.

Securing Entryways

High-quality locks and solid doors are the front line of home security.

Burglars like to get into the house the same way you do—by walking through the door. That's the easiest way for them to get items out, too. High-quality doors and locks make unwanted entry difficult and time-consuming—two things no burglar likes. Just the sight of a solid door and high-quality lock can be enough to make a thief walk away.

▶ Door and lock manufacturers have learned that many homeowners want a front entryway that's both inviting to family and guests and a deterrent to burglars. That means you have plenty of styles and options to choose from.

Look beyond the main front and back doors and secure *all* your exterior entryways. Service doors from the garage to garden, French doors to a second-story bedroom, old cellar and coal chute doors, and doors to three-season porches or conservatories should all be made as secure as possible.

Certain interior doors deserve as much protection because they function as exterior doors. The door from an attached garage to the house, and the door from the basement to the first floor are interior doors that a burglar can use to get into the main living area of the house.

Be sure all the components of your home's entryways—frame, nearby windows, and surrounding walls—are secure; one weak spot is all a thief needs to gain entry.

Screening Visitors

Amazingly, burglars often gain entry to a home simply by walking through unlocked doors or crawling through open windows. So get in the habit of keeping doors and windows closed and locked.

If you like having the door open to let in fresh air when you're home, install a screen door with a lock. Although a burglar could cut through the screen, cutting makes noise. If he can hear that someone is home, he'll likely move on if the screen is locked. With an unlocked door, he could steal a few items without making enough noise to be detected.

Securing an
Entry Door

If your exterior doors function well and look presentable, checking them isn't likely to be at the top of your to-do list. But for improved security, take a few minutes to evaluate the doors on your home.

☐ **Determine the door's composition.** If it's a hollow-core door, replace it. A hollow-core door is very easily broken through. If you can't afford to replace it, add a deadbolt near the lockset.

Doors made of solid wood usually provide adequate security—if they are in good condition. Consider *thickness* (under 1¾ inches is too thin and won't stand up to a strong kick), *age* (check for signs of deterioration and make necessary repairs), and *pattern* (floating panels can allow the door to break if kicked; solid facades with little or no decoration are best).

Many newer wood doors are actually surfaced with wood panels or pressed-wood look-alike composites and have a reinforced solid core between. These offer both the security of a new, solid-core door and the beauty of wood.

Metal-clad doors provide the most security. Steel—plain or pressed to look like a wood panel—is attached to a solid wood frame and a fiber core. These doors are strong, weatherproof, and low-maintenance.

☐ **Reinforce the frame.** If the gap between door and frame is more than 1/16th of an inch or if the door gives when pushed or moves from side to side when pried, reinforce the frame (see page 19). Gap and play allow room for a pry bar to be slipped in and the door worked open. Also, check for rot, especially around the lock. Rotting framework should be replaced even if the door and lock are sound.

▲ *The old wood doors and flimsy screen doors had to go* (inset above). *A stylish metal-clad door with shatterproof sidelights greatly improves security, updates the look of the home, and lets more sunlight in* (upper right).

☐ **Check windows and sidelights.** Any glass on the door or within arm's reach of the lock or lockset (about 40 inches) should be made of shatterproof plastic or security glass. Within that distance, a burglar can easily break ordinary glass, reach in, and open the door in a few seconds. Most new sliding glass, French, and glass-panel doors are double-paned and made of suitable materials. With the notable exception of laminated glass, you can replace most glass panes yourself (see page 35). If your door has decorative glass, install a protective panel of shatterproof plastic behind it, or sandwich it between two layers of safety glass.

Simple Ways to Secure Doors

Even the best doors can be made more secure. Improving the security of your doors requires a few tools, simple hardware and a little time.

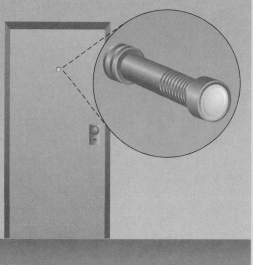

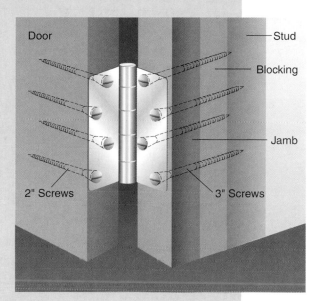

▲ Install peepholes on windowless exterior doors. Be sure you can see down to the welcome mat and out to both sides. The larger the barrel of the peephole, the more light. And that makes for a brighter, clearer view.

◄ Reinforce the door frame by inserting wood blocks, nailed in place, between the wall stud and the door frame. Gently remove interior molding, and install blocking at several points along the frame, especially where the hinges attach.

▲ Strengthen door and frame hardware by replacing any short screws on hinges with ones at least 2 inches long for the door side and at least 3 inches long for the frame side. Be sure screws that go into the frame seat firmly into studs.

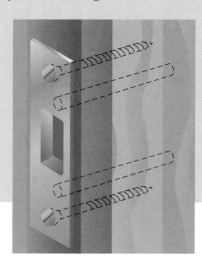

◄ Replace the strike plate with a high-security model, like the one shown here, installed with 3-inch wood screws that go deep into the frame. The steel rods, welded to the back of the strike plate, penetrate the stud and help prevent the door from being kicked in.

Securing
Special Doors

Sliding glass doors and doors that swing to the outside are options many homeowners prefer. If you choose one of these doors, you'll want to take extra precautions to keep it secure.

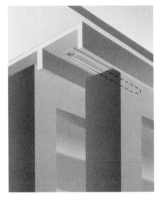

▲ *To prevent a burglar from forcing a sliding glass door, insert a steel pin into a hole drilled through the inside door frame and part way into the outside frame. Be sure to drill at least ⅝ inch away from the glass to avoid damaging glass that extends into the frame. Placing a broomstick in the bottom track can also foil an intruder.*

▲ *Some thieves just lift sliding glass doors (and windows) right out of their tracks. When the door is closed, these strong metal spacers won't let them get off the ground. With the sliding door open, position the plates (two per door) in the upper track and screw them into predrilled holes. (See also page 33.)*

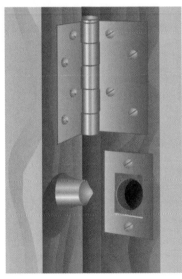

▲ *Double doors— each of them— must be firmly secured, but in different ways. Treat the door receiving most of the traffic as you would any hinged exterior door. Make the other secure by installing bar or barrel bolts at the top and bottom.*

▲ *With out-swinging doors, a burglar can pull the hinge pins free and work the door out of its opening. Prevent this by installing metal door pins like the one shown here. The protruding steel pin fits into the door frame when the door is closed, preventing the door from being pried away from the frame.*

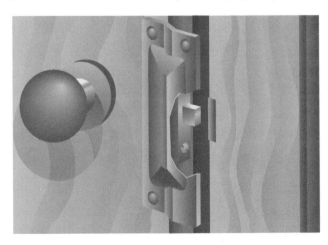

◀ *If a door swings to the outside, its latch or bolt is not protected by a stop along the jamb. A metal guard, fastened to the door with one-way screws or other hard-to-remove hardware can solve the problem. The cut-away on the side of the guard shows how it completely covers the latch, so a thief can't hacksaw or jimmy it.*

▲ *A heavy-duty lock, like this keyed version, mounts with "one-way" screws on the outer frame of the inside of a sliding glass door (at either the top or bottom). Holes drilled at intervals let you keep the door locked and partly open at the same time for ventilation and access for pets.*

Interior Doors

For added security, install solid-core interior doors with dead-bolt locks on bedroom doors, or on a door that separates the living area from the bedrooms. It's one more barrier for an intruder, and it buys you time to call police—and for them to arrive—if someone breaks in during the night.

New Doors in Old Spaces

Replacing an exterior door is a job you may be able to do yourself. It's more awkward than difficult, but having at least one other person on the job is a necessity. Here are some other things to keep in mind in choosing and installing a door:

□ **Determine door swing.** If the knob is on the left when the door swings toward you, that's a left-hand door swing. Your new door should swing in the same direction.

□ **Width is crucial.** The new door may be a different width than the old one. If the replacement is narrower, you'll have to make up the difference. Use stock whose width matches your existing framing and have it cut to the thickness that will make the rough opening match the installation directions.

Enlarging the opening can be trickier. The framing will need to be recut, and electrical circuits for lighting may have to be moved. If that's the case, you may want to hire the job out.

□ **Check the floor.** In some older homes, doors were not set on the subfloor, so once you remove the door frame you may see the joists. If so, build a base for the new door by screwing pressure-treated 2×4s to the joists.

□ **Check the height, too.** Standard, prehung replacement doors measure between $82\frac{1}{2}$ and $83\frac{1}{2}$ inches in height. Again, filling in for a smaller door is fairly easy; a taller door requires a new header—a job that may be better left to a contractor.

□ **Assemble tools and supplies before you begin.** This is one job you need to finish in a day! Gathering everything ahead of time helps ensure you can do so.

□ **Use extra care in removing interior molding.** Use a nail set and hammer to drive nails through molding (only part way if it's thicker than $\frac{1}{2}$ inch). Place a thin piece of scrap under the pry bar to protect the wall, then pry carefully. You needn't be as concerned about the exterior molding; new, prehung doors come with replacement molding.

□ **Check the rough opening for size, plumb and level.** Leave at least $\frac{3}{8}$ inch on each side to accommodate shims for fitting the new door. And, now is the time to reinforce the jamb, if desired.

Choosing Locks
For Doors

Given enough time and the right tools, just about anyone can eventually break or force a good lock. The key word here is *eventually*. The National Crime Prevention Institute says intruders generally will work no longer than 60 seconds to gain entry. Quality hardware takes longer than that to crack, so most thieves avoid strong locks. The first indicator of strength is the type of lock. Pictured here are examples of different types of locks, along with information on how they're best used.

Incidentally, burglars rarely pick locks. Why take the time when they can slip the latch, strip out a poorly made lock with a screwdriver, or pry the door open? Be sure to choose the best locks you can afford and be sure all locks are properly installed.

Look for locks made with solid metal components. For example, the bolt of a dead bolt should be solid as should the key cylinder. That makes the lock heavy, so just picking one up gives you an idea of its strength. And locks with steel components provide added strength.

Think in multiples, too. Most doors are outfitted with key-in-knob locks that are insufficient by themselves. Add a dead-bolt lock, and have one of the locks rekeyed by a locksmith to a single key for convenience and security. Or, you can buy combination sets that are designed to work on a single key and look good, too.

Working With a Locksmith

You'll find plenty of good locks that you can install without special tools, or you can hire a locksmith to help select and install locks. To find a locksmith in your area, contact The Associated Locksmiths of America, Inc., 3003 Live Oak St., Dallas, TX 75204; 214/827-1701.

▲ **Dead bolts** *let you add security without replacing an existing key-in-knob lockset. A dead bolt should have a rectangular bolt with at least a 1-inch throw into the door frame. A single cylinder deadbolt opens with a key from the outside and a knob from the inside; a double cylinder model requires a key on both sides.*

▲ **Key-in-knob locks** *offer the least protection. Many have a simple beveled spring latch that can be slipped open by inserting a credit card between the door and frame. Better key-in-knob sets include a separate tongue to help prevent that. Use these only as an extra measure of security or on interior doors.*

▲ **Chain locks** *make sense only as supplements to a good dead bolt or other lock. They let you open a door far enough to see who's there. Mount the retainer with screws long enough to penetrate the jamb studs.*

▲ **Keyless locks** let you forget about keys. And if you think someone has learned the combination, you can change it easily.

▲ **Vertical dead bolt locks** make it impossible for an intruder to gain entry with a pry bar forced between the door and frame—a tactic that works with many horizontal deadbolts. The fingers on a vertical dead bolt won't separate if pried.

Key Concepts

Where are all the keys to the house? Sure, everyone in the family has a set, but are there extra keys that can leave you vulnerable? These tips will help you account for your keys.

☐ Keep track of all keys to your house. If you give a key to a neighbor, pet sitter, or housekeeper, anyone with access to their home can take your key. Be sure the key isn't marked with your name and address. Teach children to keep track of their keys, too.

☐ Rekey the locks when you move into a new home. Even if the former owners turn over all keys in their possession, other copies may be around. Protect yourself by having a locksmith rekey all exterior locks. Also, reprogram the combination of your garage door opener (see page 27).

☐ Never hide an extra key anywhere outside your home. If losing your keys is a concern, have a trusted neighbor or relative keep an extra set for you.

☐ Rekey the lock whenever one of the keys is lost. It's better to be safe than sorry.

☐ Of course, all these recommendations apply to remote keyless entry systems and automatic garage door openers, too. The transmitters that open them perform the same function as a key, and are just as vulnerable to misuse.

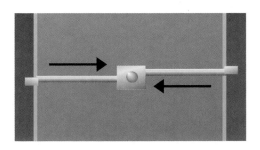

▲ **Sliding bar locks** mount in the center of a door. Turning the key or inside knob drives long dead bolts into each jamb. These are highly jimmy-resistant, and even with the hinge pins out, you can't get the door open. They're not very attractive, though, and make a clanking noise when operated. A lock like this is for high-risk locations or, perhaps, extra security on a rarely used cellar door.

Installing
Locks

Surface-Mounted Locks

Also called rim locks, surface-mounted locks have a utilitarian look, but they're a good choice if you can't bore into the door.

All surface-mounted locks depend on screws for holding power; if the screws don't penetrate at least halfway into the door, discard them and buy longer ones. For added strength, coat the screw threads with glue before driving them into pilot holes.

If an intruder could reach the lock by breaking a window, consider purchasing a double-cylinder lock that requires a key on both sides. To keep an intruder from removing the assembly, install your lock with one-way screws—they turn in but not out. Double-cylinder

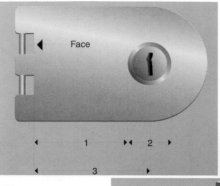

1 *To locate the distance from the door's edge to the center of the cylinder hole (3), add the distance from door edge to cylinder edge (1) to half of the cylinder diameter (2).*

2 *Attach the lock's back plate to the inside of the door. Then, draw the cylinder into the door with the mounting screws.*

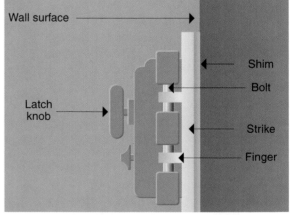

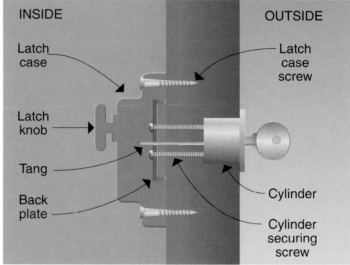

3 *Slip the latch case over the tang, drill pilot holes, and screw the latch case to the door. The tang allows you a little leeway.*

hardware generally includes an extra set of conventional, slotted screws; these are for trial installation. Mount the lock and strike plate with the slotted screws, make any adjustments, then withdraw the screws and replace them with the tamperproof versions.

Mount any surface lock about 8 to 10 inches higher than the existing knob set so you can see and operate it with ease. When you drill, work from one side of the door until the point of the bit just penetrates the opposite side. Then switch sides to complete the hole. This prevents the drill from splintering the door's surface.

4 *Mount the strike plate to the jamb. To make the fingers mesh smoothly with the bolt, add shims under the strike plate.*

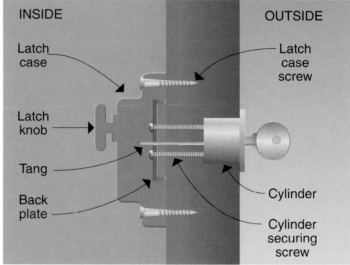

Standard Deadbolt

A standard deadbolt fits like an integral part of the door itself. Most standard deadbolts now are made so you don't have to chisel out a large section of the door, as you do for a full-mortise lock. Instead, you bore a hole through the door's face and edge, then cut a shallow recess for the bolt's faceplate and a deeper one in the jamb for the strike plate.

Before you buy a deadbolt, measure the thickness of your door. Some locks can be adjusted to compensate for doors of different thicknesses while others don't allow for adjustment; choose your new lock accordingly.

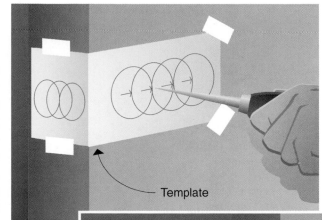

Template

1 *Like most lock hardware, deadbolt sets include a template that helps you accurately locate where to bore holes.*

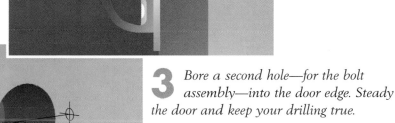

2 *Make sure you drill all holes absolutely square with the door. Use a combination square.*

3 *Bore a second hole—for the bolt assembly—into the door edge. Steady the door and keep your drilling true.*

4 *Insert the deadbolt, mark an outline for the face plate, and chisel out a recess so the plate will fit flush.*

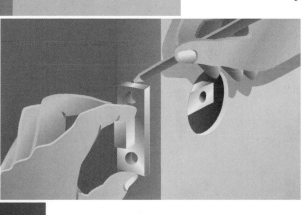

5 *Mark and cut a mortise for the strike plate. Bore the hole (and trim, if needed) to accommodate the bolt when engaged.*

Securing a
Garage

Burglars target garages for three main reasons: Garages shelter property, such as bicycles, lawn mowers, and cars, that is often easy to move and fence or strip. Most people don't spend much time in their garages, so an intruder stands a good chance of coming and going without immediate detection; and an attached garage serves as a discreet path to the rest of the house.

For openers, consider your garage door opener. It provides security because you don't have to get out of the car to open the door, and it makes it next to impossible to force the door. But if you haven't changed the electronic combination from the factory setting, your garage may be more vulnerable than you think. (See "How Secure Is Your Garage Door Opener?" on page 27.)

And what about the garage door itself? If any of its panels are loose, damaged, or inadequately secured, a burglar could climb inside without opening the door. The same goes for any garage-door windows, access doors, and doors leading to the house. They deserve as much attention as any other window or door in your home.

Finally, all the security in the world won't do any good if you leave your garage door open. A thief can dart inside and make off with items in seconds. At the very least, you're flaunting valuable equipment; at the most, you risk losing it.

➤ *This combination garage and woodworking shop keeps all tools under lock and key behind solid cabinet doors. A burglar who knows of a treasure trove of unprotected tools may even line up a buyer before he steals them.*

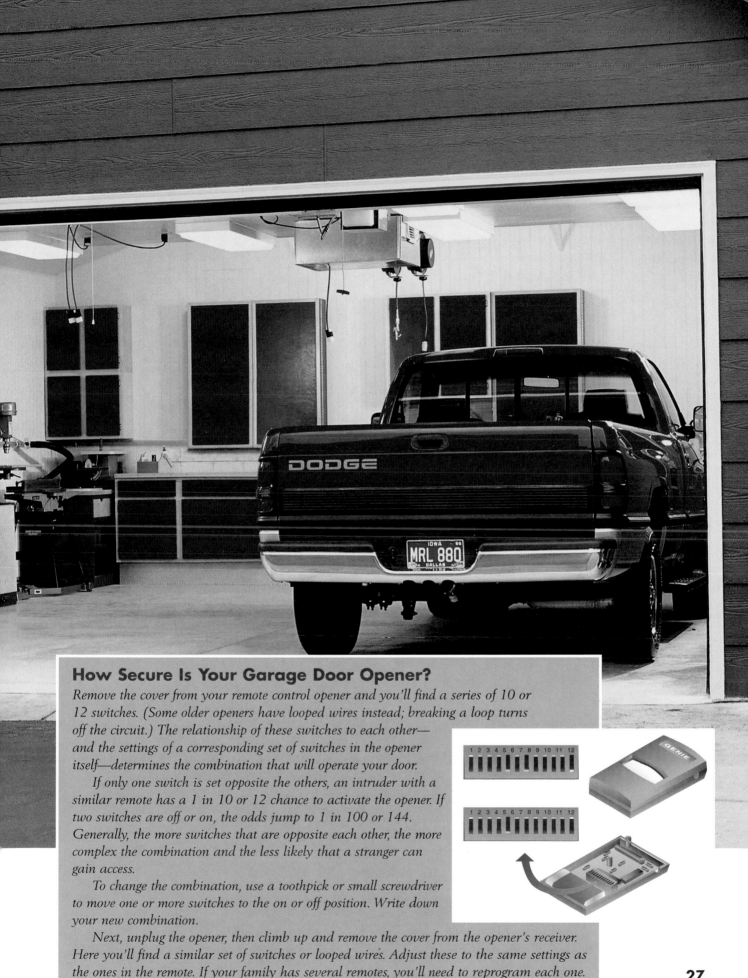

How Secure Is Your Garage Door Opener?

Remove the cover from your remote control opener and you'll find a series of 10 or 12 switches. (Some older openers have looped wires instead; breaking a loop turns off the circuit.) The relationship of these switches to each other—and the settings of a corresponding set of switches in the opener itself—determines the combination that will operate your door.

If only one switch is set opposite the others, an intruder with a similar remote has a 1 in 10 or 12 chance to activate the opener. If two switches are off or on, the odds jump to 1 in 100 or 144. Generally, the more switches that are opposite each other, the more complex the combination and the less likely that a stranger can gain access.

To change the combination, use a toothpick or small screwdriver to move one or more switches to the on or off position. Write down your new combination.

Next, unplug the opener, then climb up and remove the cover from the opener's receiver. Here you'll find a similar set of switches or looped wires. Adjust these to the same settings as the ones in the remote. If your family has several remotes, you'll need to reprogram each one.

Securing
Windows

Window shopping is a favorite pastime for many burglars.

Inadequately protected windows are easy marks for intruders who know how to force them without too much effort.

Fortunately, reinforcing windows in your home is neither difficult nor expensive. Most measures require just a little skill, a few basic tools, and the right hardware.

Evaluating Windows

First, survey the windows of your house. Check out each for its ability to withstand an attack, paying special attention to basement windows and any windows that can be reached from ground level. Then list each on paper, noting its type and the locking mechanism currently securing it.

Keep in mind that you'll need to replace the original locks on most windows with sturdy, reliable ones. For example, ordinary sash locks on double-hung windows squeeze out drafts, but provide little security. An intruder can simply insert a knife up between the sashes and turn the lock to its open position, or exert enough pressure to snap the hardware. You'll get better protection for double-hung windows with the devices illustrated on pages 30-31.

➤ *An abundance of windows brings in plenty of sunlight and fresh air. Left open and unattended, however, something undesirable can get in, too. Make sure the windows all around your house are closed and locked when no one is home.*

Windows don't always have to be closed to shut out potential thieves. Some locks allow you to secure a window in a partly open position for ventilation. No matter how your windows are secured, whether they're locked or fastened shut in some other manner, consider how you and your family could exit them in an emergency. And if you install locks, keep the keys nearby and make sure everyone knows where they are.

What good are window locks if an intruder can simply break the glass to get in? Glass is somewhat of a deterrent in its own right because it slows an intruder down and the broken shards have the potential to injure, but shattering glass attracts the kind of attention burglars don't want. If you don't feel secure about glass, replace it with impact-resistant acrylic or polycarbonate, or high-security glass. Another (although less attractive) alternative is to install a metal grille outside the window or a scissors gate inside. Some gates have quick-release levers for emergency exits, but a stationary grille renders a window useless as a fire exit.

New Windows

If you're replacing windows or adding new windows, be sure to ask about built-in security features. For example, you may be able to upgrade the security of the window with stronger locks, laminated glass, or built-in sensors. You may pay a little more but you won't have to add a desired feature later.

Locks for Double-Hung Windows

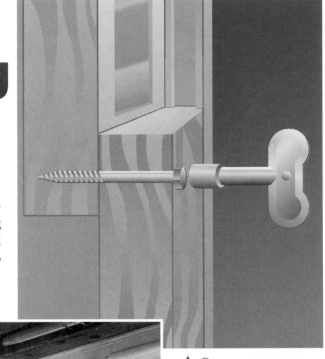

Even though they are extremely popular, double-hung windows just aren't terribly secure. Making them secure isn't complicated or expensive, and all but one of the methods listed here allow you to keep the window partially open.

▲ *One way to secure double-hung windows is to install an inexpensive lag-screw system.*

Pre-drill the sashes and insert the screws through recessed washers. Tighten the screws with a special key provided with the hardware. Make sure the screws don't go clear through the upper sash— they'll let in outside air.

Another hole or two on the upper sash lets you lock the window in partly open positions for ventilation.

Every Window Counts
Remember to secure garage and shed windows, too. And cover them with curtains or blinds. They may not wow neighbors with your interior design savvy, but window treatments make it all but impossible for prowlers to scope what you've stored inside.

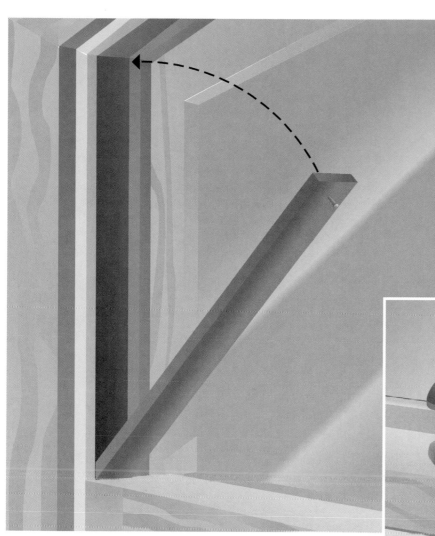

◄ Here's an even easier way to protect double-hung windows. With this method, you don't have to purchase any special hardware. Cut a piece of scrap wood and wedge it inside the channel that runs/operates the lower sash. Of course this isn't as tidy, and you can't secure the window in a partially open position.

◄ Another protective measure for double-hung windows features a keyed lock with a lever. Center it on the top rail of the bottom sash, the same place the original latch was installed.

◄ A bolt-action, keyed lock also strengthens double-hung windows. Install it on the top rail of the bottom sash, flush to one side of the upper sash. Keep the key near enough for quick emergency exits, but out of reach of a prowler's exploring hand. To secure windows in an open position and provide ventilation, install additional brackets on the upper sash.

Locks for Casement Windows

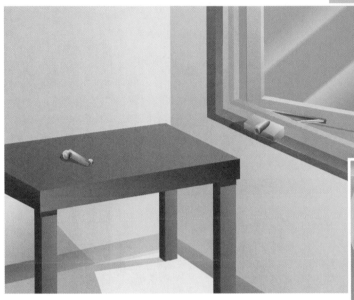

▲ *Many casement windows won't open enough to admit an adult. To check, fully open the sash and measure the clearance. If it's less than 6½ inches, only a very slim person could squeeze in.*

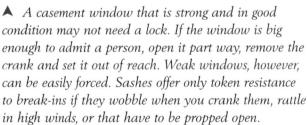

▲ *A casement window that is strong and in good condition may not need a lock. If the window is big enough to admit a person, open it part way, remove the crank and set it out of reach. Weak windows, however, can be easily forced. Sashes offer only token resistance to break-ins if they wobble when you crank them, rattle in high winds, or that have to be propped open.*

▲ *If you prefer a lock and key, choose a casement window lock similar to this one. Use screws to install it along the sash rail. Keep the key nearby so you can get out in an emergency.*

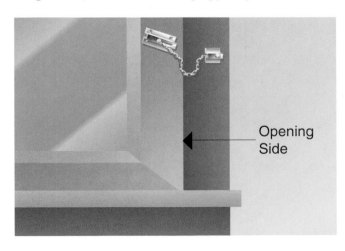

Opening Side

◄ *The same chain locks used with doors can keep windows from opening more than a few inches, just enough to let in a breath of fresh air. Fasten it to the sash and frame with the longest screws the sashes will accommodate.*

Locks for
Sliding Windows

◄ *Savvy burglars have an easy time prying open poorly protected sliding windows. With only a little pressure, they can snap the brittle metal catch that holds the window closed. Stop them by inserting a metal clip into the lower track and against the closed window. The clip can be bent by hand to adjust to channel thickness.*

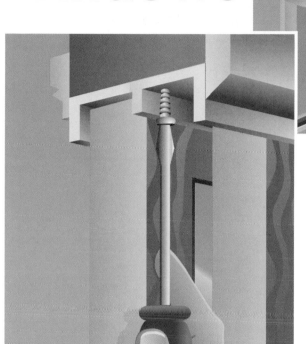

▲ *Most sliding windows lift up and out of their tracks with little effort. Prevent intruders from entering by driving sheet metal screws part way into the upper track. Adjust the screws so the window just clears them when it slides, leaving no room to maneuver the window from its track.*

▲ *A Charley bar also provides all the holding power needed to stop an intruder from prying open a sliding window. Easy to install with just a few screws, the bar can be raised when it's not being used and held by a clip in the "up" position. The bar protects against prying, but doesn't preclude jimmying the unit up and out of the track.*

◄ *Sturdy lock-and-key sets are another way to secure sliding windows. To install, drill holes in the windowsill for the screws as shown. Then fasten the lock in place. To secure windows in a partially open position, drill another set of holes in the sill at the desired spot. (This type of lock also works on vertical sliding windows.)*

Protecting
Basement
Windows

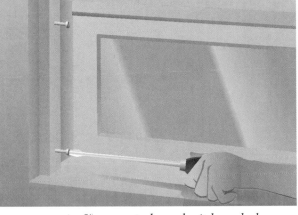

▲ Scissors-type gates and sturdy hinged metal shutters can be padlocked from the inside yet opened easily when desired. Be sure to keep keys nearby but out of sight—and reach—from the outside.

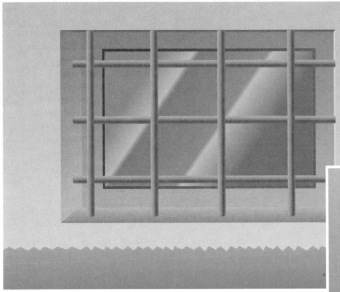

▲ Standard or custom-made grilles mortared into the foundation give basement windows a behind-bars look—but they provide peace of mind in high-crime areas. For even more security, use glass blocks to wall up the openings completely. Both of these methods, of course, eliminate being able to exit by the window.

▲ If your windows don't have locks, drive long screws into a stop on either side at a height that will allow the window to open a few inches. This tactic also rules out using the window as an emergency exit.

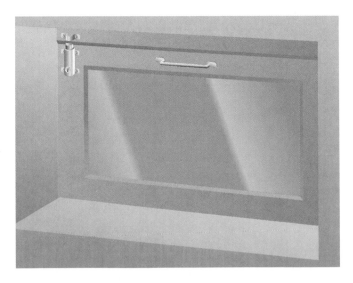

◄ Thwart break-in attempts by installing a sturdy hasp and keyed padlock. Keep the key nearby (but out of reach from the outside) so you can easily open the window for ventilation or in case it's needed in an emergency.

Window Glass
Alternatives

Burglars traditionally don't like to break glass because it makes too much noise, but you can't expect every prowler to stand on tradition. If a window can't be forced open, intruders have been known to stick tape to a pane, break it, and quietly pull away the pieces to create an opening.

To improve the security of your windows, consider replacing the standard glass in your home's most vulnerable windows with security glazing. Alternatives to ordinary window glass fall into four categories.

☐ **Wire glass** has wire mesh embedded in it. It breaks easily but the wire holds much of the shards in place and impedes entry. It's typically used in industrial applications, but often is a good choice for basement and garage windows.

☐ **Tempered glass** is several times stronger than ordinary glass, but it will break if enough force is applied. It's commonly used in storefront windows.

☐ **Plastic glazing** is often UL-listed for resistance to blows that would shatter and destroy ordinary glass. The most common types are acrylic (such as Plexiglas™) and polycarbonate (Lexan™). Acrylic can deflect a thrown rock, but will break if hit with a hammer. Polycarbonate, which costs twice as much, is virtually indestructible. It resists heat, flames, extreme cold, hammers, picks, and axes. Both types of plastic glazing cost and weigh less than laminated glass, but are more easily scratched and defaced. They also yellow from exposure to sunlight.

Installation procedures are much the same as for glass, but ordinary glazing compound can't stand up to plastic's greater rate of expansion and contraction. Instead, use the more elastic silicone-base glazing compound.

☐ **Laminated glass**, the type used in car windows, consists of two layers of glass bonded to plastic between them. The glass will shatter into fragments, but these usually adhere to the plastic instead of falling out of the frame. Laminated glass is costly, heavy, and much thicker than other materials. It has special installation requirements, so you'll need to have a professional install it.

Reglazing Windows

Replacing glass with security glazing in a wooden sash window can be done by most homeowners. Here are a few tips:

☐ *Determine the size of your new pane (⅛-inch less in length and width than the opening).*

☐ *Chipping off old glazing compound can be the hardest part. Use a putty knife or old chisel (1); soften the old compound with a soldering iron.*

☐ *Remove the old glazier's points and scrape away the last of the old compound (2) to make a clean bed for the new compound.*

☐ *If you're using silicone compound, paint the groove; silicone won't adhere to bare wood.*

☐ *Apply a ⅛-inch-thick layer of glazing compound (3). This helps seal and cushion the pane.*

☐ *Line up one edge of the pane in the sash, lower it into place, and press gently with your fingertips to embed it in the glazing compound (4).*

☐ *Press glazier's points into the sash with a putty knife. Don't push too hard. Then apply a ¼-inch bead of glazing compound and press it into place.*

☐ *Bevel the compound with a putty knife.*

☐ *Don't paint silicone glazing compound.*

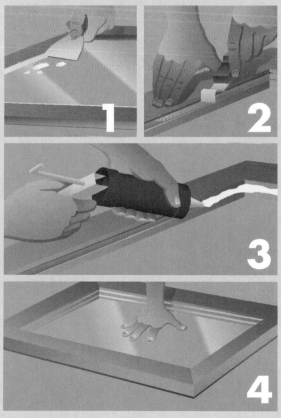

Alarm
Systems

You're sure to find the right system if you consider your family's lifestyle and budget as you review the dazzling array of options.

For centuries, the wealthiest homeowners relied on alert and trusted watchmen to guard their families and property. Today, the equivalent of such protection is available to virtually all homeowners with an alarm system. Like the watchman, the electronic eyes and ears of an alarm system are constantly scanning for any sign of an intruder. And, if an intruder is detected, the electronic watchman "shouts" an alarm to frighten off the intruder, warn the home's occupants, and summon assistance. Unlike its human counterpart, the modern alarm system often is relatively inexpensive, never falls asleep, can't be bribed, and is unintimidated by even the most fearsome of intruders.

Electronic alarm systems are powerful deterrents. According to the National Burglar and Fire Alarm Association, homes equipped with electronic alarm systems are roughly three times less likely to be broken into than those without. Many insurance companies, noting that fewer break-ins mean fewer claims, offer discounts from 5 to 15 percent on homeowners' insurance premiums for homes with alarm systems.

Is an alarm system right for you? With systems for as little as $100, and portable alarms for even less, most people who want alarms can find something that will work for them. Remember that these systems are only a part of good home security. Solid doors and locks and the rest of the basics of home security, are still important. And just like locks, electronic alarm systems have to be used properly to be effective. Choose a system that fits your budget and your lifestyle.

Alarm System Basics

A basic electronic alarm system is a low-voltage electrical circuit with sensors installed on doors and windows. When the flow of electricity through one of those sensors is interrupted because the door or window is opened, a warning signal goes off—a siren sounds or a light flashes. Many systems also include motion sensors that cover large areas. When something moves within a sensor's range, an alarm sounds. Some systems are monitored systems—they send a signal to a central station where operators, in turn, notify police.

Residential electronic alarm systems come in two basic types: wired and wireless. As the name implies, wired systems require running low-voltage electrical wires from a master control panel to sensors on doors and windows, motion detectors, keypads, and sirens. The wires are usually concealed inside walls and in crawl spaces. Professional installers use special tools and have developed methods for getting the wires through the tiniest spaces. They can hide wires and sensors to make the system as inconspicuous as possible.

Wireless systems use miniature radio transmitters instead of wires to send signals between the main control panel and the sensors, so very little drilling and no special tools are required for instal-

Yard Signs and Window Stickers

An important value of having an electronic security system is its deterrent value—which you can increase with warning decals. Place them on windows around your house and put a yard sign in the yard: They will be seen by anyone scoping out the neighborhood.

lation. Wireless systems have the additional advantage of mobility: You can easily remove a wireless system and take it with you when you move. Security companies install both types of systems. If you want to do the installation yourself, the simplicity of the installation makes a wireless system a better choice for most homeowners.

Both wired and wireless systems can be enhanced with a variety of options—from motion detectors that aren't tripped by pets to remote access that allows you to check the system from a touch-tone phone anywhere. It's easy to get dazzled by the options and buy more than you'll need or use. Start by assessing what you want the basic system to protect.

Intercoms

By itself or as part of an electronic alarm system, an intercom is one of the most cost-effective home security devices. With it, you can communicate with someone at the door from a safe distance—even out of view of the person—control a buzzer-latch on your gate, monitor a baby or child's room, or even pipe music through the house.

Intercoms vary in complexity, but all operate on low voltages, stepped down via a transformer from your home's electrical system. This makes them relatively easy and safe to install. Pay close attention to the instructions that come with the system, however, to ensure your safety.

Unless you are working with new construction, your biggest challenge will be unobtrusively routing or fishing wires from one room to another. With flush-mounted wall components, you also will have to cut into walls but probably won't have to alter the framing.

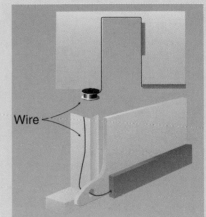

Wire

◄ *Low-voltage wiring is similar to that used for telephones. Often you can run it along moldings.*

VOLUME   SPEAK   LISTEN

◄ *Substations have a combined speaker and microphone with switches that transfer from listen to talk modes.*

1 2 3

▲ *The master station contains circuitry that lets you call any or all of the substations. It may also include a radio.*

▲ *Outdoor substations often include a button to sound the doorbell or chimes.*

Planning Your Alarm System

Levels of Protection

The goal of a residential security system is to detect an intruder as early as possible, alert the home's occupants of his presence, and scare him away before he does any harm. Creating progressive layers of protection accomplishes this goal. Imagine four concentric circles in and around your house, with your family and your most valuable possessions inside the center circle. The interior of your home is the second layer, the exterior shell of your home (often called its "perimeter" by home-security specialists) is the third, and the property surrounding your home is the fourth.

For most people, installing a security system that protects the second and third circles (the interior and shell of the house) is both effective and cost efficient. That third circle, the exterior shell or points of entry of your home, is the place to install your first line of defense. This layer of protection consists of alarm sensors on the windows and exterior doors. You may want to install alarm screens so you can leave windows open but still protected and glassbreak sensors to detect any attempt to break the glass out of a window or sliding glass door.

Strategically placed interior motion detectors are the second layer of protection and serve as backup to the point-of-entry protection. Protecting the interior is especially important if you don't install a complete point-of-entry system. Should an intruder slip through, an interior motion detector will activate the alarm as soon as he enters its field. At a minimum, include motion detectors in central walkways, hallways, entry areas, or family rooms. A more thorough interior protection would include motion detectors in all rooms that contain valuables, such as the master bedroom, dining room, family room, and home office. Remember that motion detectors don't discern between you, the

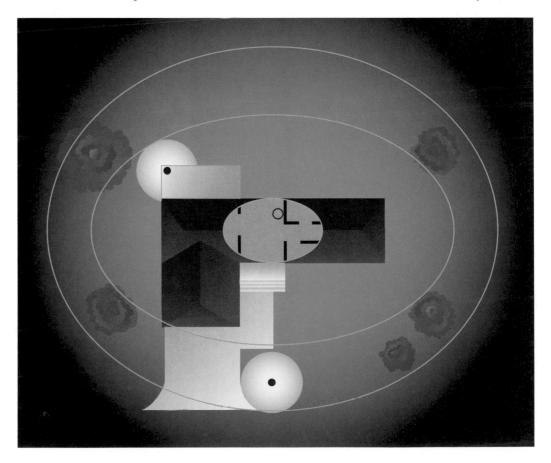

family dog, or an intruder; any change in the infrared field trips the alarm. The type and placement of motion detectors is critical—and so is remembering to turn the system off when people are home to avoid accidentally tripping the alarm. Some motion detectors can be set to allow pets to have free run of the house.

The innermost circle requires spot protection for high-value areas, such as a security closet, safe, or gun cabinet; this circle also includes 24-hour panic buttons. Spot protection is often controlled separately and can remain on even when the rest of the system is turned off. A 24-hour panic button is always on and can be pressed at any time to sound the alarm and, if the system is monitored, summon help from the central station. Panic buttons are located on each of the system's keypads and also are available in portable versions that slip on a key chain, clip onto a belt, or can be worn as a pendant.

The outermost circle of protection consists of motion sensors to let you know when someone has come onto your property. Unless you have a large amount of land surrounding your home, or you live in a remote or hidden location, this type of protection is likely more than you need for the cost involved.

Once you determine how many layers of protection you need, decide how you want your security system to respond. At a minimum, include one interior alarm siren to scare off the burglar and alert you to the situation. Large houses may need a second interior siren. You may want to add an exterior siren, heard outside your house, so the neighbors will know when your alarm is activated. Also, consider whether or not you want the system monitored by a UL-listed central station.

How Much Do You Need?

Are you mainly concerned about protecting your possessions when no one's home? Then a basic system protecting exterior doors and one or two interior traps may be sufficient. An intruder may be able to enter through a window, but will trip the alarm when he comes within range of a trap—a motion detector. This is the least expensive type of system, and with professional installation typically

Fire Protection

If your system is a monitored system, including one or more smoke detectors is a good idea. System smoke detectors are different from those that came with your house or are sold at the hardware store. They provide superior fire protection because you can select specific kinds of fire sensors for the kitchen, laundry room, garage, and sleeping areas; you won't have dead smoke detectors because you forgot to replace the batteries; and, if your system is monitored, it can summon the fire department even if no one is home when the fire breaks out.

costs from $100 to $1,000, depending on whether you lease or purchase it and whether it will be monitored. (See "Buying or Leasing—Who Owns Your Alarm System?" page 45.) If you have a very large home or own extremely valuable or irreplaceable items, include additional motion detectors to cover the areas in which you keep them.

If you add round-the-clock monitoring by a UL-listed central station; monitoring typically costs between $15 and $30 per month, in addition to the cost of the hardware and installation.

If you're primarily concerned with protecting yourself and your family when you're home, you'll want a complete perimeter system. The goal is to have the system detect an intruder before he actually enters your home, and frighten him off with a loud siren. Alarm sensors are installed on all exterior doors and openable windows. The cost of a complete perimeter system is directly related to the number of doors and windows protected. For professional installation, plan to spend $1,000 to $2,000 for the basic equipment plus $50 to $100 for each protected door and window.

Get bids from two or three reputable security companies in your area. Listen to the recommendations of the different sales reps, and ask plenty of questions. This will help you to decide what features you want and which ones you can live without. Also, check with your insurance agent to see if you'll receive a discount on your homeowner's insurance if you install a certain type of system.

The Elements
of an Alarm System

All home security systems are comprised of several key components: a master control panel, at least one keypad, and a selection of sensors. Think about where these components can be placed in your home for maximum effectiveness. Here's an overview of each component.

Master Control Panel

This is the brains of the system. The CPU (Central Processing Unit) receives information from the alarm sensors and keypads and decides when to sound the sirens or call the central station. Be sure to select a master control panel with enough capacity to handle all the sensors you install now and those you may add in the future. The control panel also contains a backup battery to power the system for several hours in case your electricity goes out. For hard-wired systems, the control panel is usually a wall-mounted metal cabinet located in a closet or the basement.

Keypad

The keypad is the system's command center. From it, you control the system's every function—arming and disarming, silencing the siren, and reviewing past alarm activity and other functions. Most keypads have numbered buttons, a buzzer, and a digital display panel. Some even speak with an electronic voice. To operate the system, you enter a code, then follow the instructions on the display. The buzzer reminds you to turn off the system when you arrive home. Most keypads also have a panic button that can be pressed at any time to sound the alarm and, in monitored systems, send an emergency signal to the central station.

Since you'll be using the keypad to turn your system on and off as you exit and enter the house, install one just inside your most frequently used door (usually the one leading to the garage). If convenience dictates and your budget allows, consider adding keypads in the front entry area and in the master bedroom.

Door and Window Sensors —
Magnetic Contacts

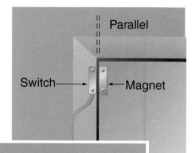

A break in the magnetic contact trips the alarm when the door or window is opened. Some magnetic contacts are concealed within the frames of door or window frames. Others are small, plastic devices that mount on the surface of door and window frames. For entry doors, an entry/exit delay is programmed into the system to allow you time to enter and leave through specified doors without setting off the alarm.

Alarm
Screens

These replace the insect screens on openable windows and are almost identical in appearance to regular screens. The alarm is tripped if the screen is cut or removed from the window frame. Alarm screens are the most expensive type of window sensor, but they protect the entire window opening—even when the window is open.

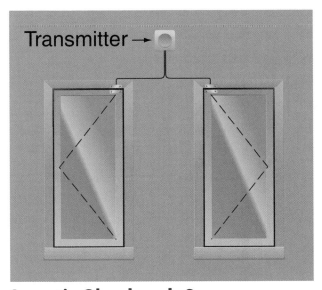

Transmitter →

Acoustic Glassbreak Sensors

A determined intruder can get around a door or window sensor by breaking out the glass and crawling through—without actually opening anything. Acoustic glassbreak sensors will, however, detect such an intrusion. Small electronic devices activate the alarm when they "hear" the unique sound frequencies generated by breaking glass. One acoustic glassbreak sensor will typically cover all the windows in a large room. Some glassbreak sensors are designed to mount on the window frame and have a built-in magnetic contact to detect either the window being opened or the glass being broken.

Motion Sensors

A passive infrared motion sensor—PIR—is the most common type. This miniature electronic device is a low-cost, reliable unit that detects body heat, and is usually mounted in a corner of the room near the ceiling. As a rule, PIRs should be located so that no object that rapidly changes temperature is within its field of view. Be sure to direct it away from heater vents, wood stoves, and sun-heated windows as their temperature changes can set off false alarms. A PIR sensor is most effective at detecting a person walking across its field of view as opposed to directly toward or away from the unit. So, mount the unit where anyone entering the room will cross the sensor's field. Most rooms can be effectively covered by a single PIR unit. If your pets have a free run of the house, choose pet-immune motion sensors.

Sirens and Strobes

Interior sirens are usually small devices designed for surface mounting on an interior wall. When the alarm is activated, the interior siren sounds both to warn those at home and to scare off the intruder. Exterior sirens alert the neighbors and discourage the intruder before entering the house. Most sirens included in fire-protection systems produce one sound for an intrusion and another very different sound for a fire. You can program how long the alarm sounds, so after a preset amount of time, it will quit. The system will automatically reset.

Strobe lights are another option that you can install to alert you, the neighbors, and the police of a break-in. Mounted on the front of the house, the strobe flashes brightly during an alarm, discouraging the intruder, and making it easy for the police to find the right house. Strobes in fire systems will also flash when the fire alarm is triggered, so the fire department can readily identify your house even if the fire is contained in a small area. As an added advantage, the strobe can be set to continue flashing after your siren shuts off. That way, if you're away from home, you'll know that your alarm was activated as you approach the house.

Portable Alarms

If you don't want to install a full system, or don't have a good place to mount a motion sensor, consider using a portable alarm. These small, battery-operated, self-contained units are motion sensor and alarm in one. Some styles sit on a flat surface, such as a table or shelf, others hang on the door knob. They are good choices for apartments and for added security in hotel rooms.

The Elements
of an Alarm System

Outdoor Protection

Including outdoor protection in your system adds an "early warning" feature. Placed strategically around your property, electronic sensors send a signal to the house to let you know when someone is coming. Since many things can trigger these sensors, connect them to a chime or buzzer in the house, rather than directly to the alarm of your security system. You may also want the sensors to turn on floodlights, activate a recorded voice warning, or even to switch on miniature surveillance cameras. Types of outdoor sensors include:

☐ **Outdoor passive infrared—PIR—motion detectors** that cover an area of about 60 by 60 feet, and are good for patios, courtyards, porches, and parking areas. Some models are designed to ignore small animals to minimize false alarms.

☐ **Photoelectric beams** which send an invisible beam from a transmitter to a receiver located up to 500 feet away, and detect anyone or anything crossing the beam.

☐ **Stress sensors** that are tiny devices that attach to the underside of wooden decks, stairs, or balconies and send a signal when the wood flexes from the weight of anyone stepping on it.

☐ **Driveway sensors** that can detect any car that pulls in your driveway.

☐ **Surveillance cameras** that are installed above exterior doors and around the property allow you to observe your property from inside your home. These cameras can be hooked up to a television set or to a separate monitor.

Special Features

You can customize many high-end electronic security systems to make the operation more convenient, and to better suit your lifestyle and home protection needs. Because the installation and pro-

gramming for many of these features is complex, you will likely only be able to get the features if you buy a professionally installed system. Here are a few specialized options you may want to consider.

☐ **Smoke and heat detectors.** These work like other smoke and heat detectors with a few additional benefits: no batteries to worry about, the alarm siren is louder than sirens on smoke and heat detectors, and if you have a central monitoring service, they send a call for help as soon as the alarm is triggered.

☐ **Custom English display.** A small display screen at each keypad can be used to check the status of your system. Each sensor is named in English abbreviations—*Master Bedrm Window, Ft Hall Smoke Det*—rather than by number or other code.

☐ **Chime mode.** When the system is disarmed, the opening of a window or an exterior door signals the keypads throughout the house to emit a chime tone.

☐ **Automatic paging.** The system pages you when the alarm has been tripped or when a special "event" happens. For example, it lets you know when a child has returned home from school.

☐ **Automatic shut-off and reset.** Another way to allow access to your home at preset times is to choose a system that allows automatic shutoff times. That way, the system will be disarmed when kids get home from school. You can also program some systems to reset later. If you're on vacation, for example, the system could be set to allow a "window" of access for a pet sitter or caretaker.

☐ **Lights.** You can send the system a signal from your car as you drive up, or by phone before you head home, so the interior and exterior of your home will be lit when you arrive. You can also program the system to turn on lights when the alarm is triggered.

☐ **Codeless on and off.** If remembering the number code to activate and deactivate the system is a problem, the system can be "keyed" with an electronic card or key fob. Placing the card near the keypad turns the system on or off.

☐ **Event log.** The simplest of these notes, in order of the occurrence, the zone or device that was tripped. The most sophisticated logs the exact time and date of every activity (event), including who turned the system on and off.

☐ **Remote operation.** You can call your system from a touch-tone phone and, by entering a special code, check the system or change features.

☐ **Remote programming and diagnostics.** This feature allows your alarm company to test and service your system from the office, saving time and expensive service calls.

☐ **Special codes for occasional users.** Using different codes or key cards, the system allows and records entry for different people. For example, "regular users" are household members who can come and go all the time. However, the codes or key cards for "occasional users," such as housekeepers or baby-sitters, are programmed to allow these people access only on preset days and times.

☐ **Duress code.** If someone follows you into your home and forces you to disable the system, keying in a special code disarms the system but sends a silent duress signal to the monitoring location.

☐ **Telephone "line cut" monitor.** If your phone line is cut, the alarm is automatically triggered.

☐ **Radio or cellular backup.** Should your phone service be interrupted, a monitored system would not be able to contact the central office. With a radio or cellular backup system, any alarm would still reach the monitoring system.

☐ **Two-way audio monitoring.** Small microphones mounted throughout the house allow the central monitoring service to listen to sounds in your home when the alarm is triggered. Small speakers allow the operator to talk to you without the phone.

☐ **"I'm OK" monitoring.** Designed for people living alone, this feature alerts the central monitoring station if the system's motion detectors don't sense any motion within a certain amount of time. Then the service calls a friend or neighbor to check on the homeowner.

Area Arming

Using different keypad commands, you activate and deactivate the system in different parts of the house. For example, you could deactivate the system for the main portion of the house, but leave it active in the office, garage, and workshop.

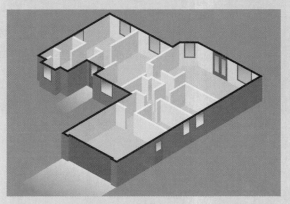

Home mode

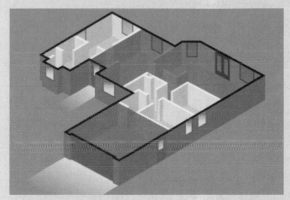

Sleep mode

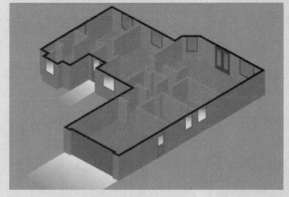

Away mode

Evaluating
Alarm Systems

Install It Yourself or Hire A Security Company

If you're handy with basic tools and written instructions, you can easily install a basic security system yourself. You'll save 50 to 60 percent over the cost of a professional installation. If you're protecting a detached garage, shop, or even a rustic cabin, you can install a hard-wired system without being too concerned about concealing the wires. Wireless systems usually are a better choice if you install a system in your home. The wireless equipment costs more than the wired version, but the time you save in running and hiding wires are worth it.

If you keep especially valuable items at home, such as fine art, jewelry, or collections, you're a can-didate for having a security system designed and installed by a professional security company. It's also wise to leave an installation for a very large home (as well as systems with lots of advanced features) to the pros. Wiring and programming large security systems can be quite complex.

Keep these two things in mind if you're thinking of installing your own home security system:

☐ National, state, and local electrical codes govern the installation of all electrical systems—including security systems. Fire codes regulate the installation of smoke detectors, especially in new construction and remodeling. These codes are in place for your safety. Make sure you become familiar with and comply with all of them. Check with your local building department to get this information.

☐ The monitoring feature of a system, should you choose it, is best installed by a qualified technician. While installing the sensors can often be done by a homeowner, connecting the system to the telephone lines and programming it to communicate with the central station are best left to someone with special training.

False Alarms

The term "false alarm" is historically applied to situations in which fire fighting equipment is dispatched to a location in which no fire is found. It also applies to cases in which police respond to a monitored security system and find no evidence of a break-in.

False alarms have become a major concern to police departments. Many report that over 90 percent of the alarm calls they respond to are false. When officers are occupied investigating false alarms, they are unavailable to handle real emergencies. As a result, many cities now fine homeowners who repeatedly produce false alarms. Fines typically range from $20 to $100, depending on the yearly number of false alarms at the property.

Why so many false alarms? The biggest cause appears to be user error. Other causes can be improper system design, poor quality equipment, improper installation, and poor maintenance.

Police acknowledge the effectiveness of security systems in deterring burglaries. So the challenge for both security companies and homeowners is to prevent false alarms. Here are some tips:

☐ Have your system installed by a reputable company. (See "Choosing a Security Company" on page 45.)
☐ If you install a system yourself, purchase quality equipment from a reputable supplier and follow the manufacturer's instructions carefully.
☐ Make sure everyone using the system is thoroughly trained. Each month, have each person practice turning the system on and off—it's easy to forget how if they use the system infrequently.
☐ If your system is monitored, post the phone number of the central station near the telephone so you can quickly call and cancel an accidental alarm.
☐ Test your system thoroughly each month. (Call the central monitoring station first and tell them you're testing so they won't send the police. When you're done, call them back to make sure they received your alarm signals, and to let them know your test is complete.)
☐ Follow your security company's or equipment supplier's recommendations for maintenance of your system. If you ever notice something isn't working properly, get it fixed immediately.

Buying or Leasing—Who Owns Your Security System?

Security companies sell or lease the equipment—CPU, keypads, sensors—of the security systems they install. Some companies base profits on the sale and installation of the equipment, with monitoring offered as an option. Other companies lease the equipment and require a 3- to 5-year lease/monitoring contract; their profit comes from your ongoing monthly payments.

That's why the up-front cost of an installed sold system is considerably higher than for an identical leased system. To attract customers, some lease-only companies advertise a $99 special, or even offer to install a basic security system at no charge. But be careful, these ultra-low-cost systems are often very basic. By the time you add the items necessary to provide adequate protection, you may pay substantially more than if you had chosen a comparable traditional installation package.

When a company sells you the equipment for a security system outright, you own it forever. Once the warranty expires, you'll have to pay for any service or maintenance required. However, if the system works just fine but you become dissatisfied with the monitoring service, you can easily change companies without replacing the equipment. If you decide to purchase your security system, insist on standard equipment that is readily accessible to other security companies, so your system will be compatible if you change it in the future.

Leased systems remain the property of the security company. Your monthly bill usually combines the fees for lease of the equipment and 24-hour monitoring. If you cancel their service, the security company can come and remove the system from your home. Security lease and monitoring contracts vary widely from company to company. Some allow you to cancel anytime, without penalty. Others obligate you to pay the entire remaining balance of the contract immediately if you cancel for any reason. Some companies charge for servicing leased systems, some don't. Read any security contract carefully and make sure you understand all the terms before you sign.

Choosing a Security Company

If you're going to have your security system professionally installed, it pays to do your homework. You'll be trusting the protection of your home and family to that company, so you'll want to have confidence in their qualifications. How do you find a qualified and reputable security company? Here's your checklist:

☐ Start by asking your friends, neighbors, and insurance agent for referrals. Find out what they liked—and didn't like—about the company they use.

☐ Contact the National Burglar & Fire Alarm Association (301/907-3202) and your state burglar and fire alarm association for a list of member companies in your area. Reputable companies will belong to one or both of these associations.

☐ Ask your state's licensing agencies, consumer protection agencies, Better Business Bureau, and your

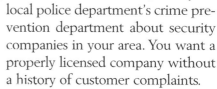

local police department's crime prevention department about security companies in your area. You want a properly licensed company without a history of customer complaints.

☐ Call several companies and ask these questions over the phone: (To avoid unwanted sales calls, don't give your name, phone number, or address on your first call. A good firm will understand your desire to protect your privacy.)

•How long have they been in business in your area? Five years or more suggests they'll be around in the future to continue servicing your system.

•Are they a licensed low-voltage electrical contractor? If your state requires a separate alarm-contractor's license, make sure they also have this license. And, ask for their license numbers so you can verify the information.

•Are they bonded and insured? Should any damage occur while they're installing your system, you'll want them to pay for repairs.

•Do they conduct background checks before hiring employees? It's an indication of professionalism if they do, and an assurance to you about the people installing and monitoring your system.

•Do they sell or lease security systems? Which is better for you depends on your home security needs. (See "Buying or Leasing—Who Owns Your Security System?" at left.)

Evaluating
Alarm Systems

•Where is the central monitoring office, and does the company own the monitoring service, too? Monitoring offices aren't necessarily local; they can be out of state, even across the country. And some companies purchase monitoring services from other companies. These are not necessarily problems; you just need to be aware.

•Is the monitoring service UL-listed? That is the key to ensuring the quality of the central station, wherever it is located.

Once you've narrowed the field to three or four security companies, set up appointments for their sales representatives to visit your home.

Ask each company's sales rep for a security inspection of your home, his or her recommendations, and a written price quote or proposal. Here are some other questions you'll want to ask the sales representative:

•How long does the company warrant the system and what does the warranty cover? Get this is writing!

•What is their hourly service rate? Is there a minimum service charge?

•Do they require a monitoring contract? If so, for how long?

•Have the salesperson leave you a blank copy of his company's contract for you to read after he or she leaves. Don't sign anything you don't understand or are not comfortable with.

•What is their monthly monitoring rate? Are there any limitations on how often and how much they can increase their rates?

•What brands of equipment do they use? Ask for a brochure or a specification sheet that lists the features of the CPU and keypads. Have the sales rep show you a sample of the keypad the company will be installing and to explain its use. Does it seem user friendly or confusing and complicated?

•Ask each sales rep for the names and phone numbers of several satisfied customers and take the time to give them a call.

•Listen to the salesperson's recommendations—a sales rep is the expert on the products and services the company sells. But, remember, most work on a commission, so the more they sell you, the more they make.

•Visit the prospective companies. You can learn a lot by seeing how they keep their own facilities. Make sure what you see matches what the salesperson said about the company—size, type of equipment in use, and, if it's on site, the central monitoring station. Be wary of any company whose salesperson says their facilities are off limits to customers.

Look for a UL Label

Underwriters Laboratories—UL—is the largest organization in the United States that provides third-party testing and safety certification of products and procedures. UL also is the primary organization setting published standards for the security industry covering equipment, security company operations, installation, testing procedures, and the operation of central monitoring stations.

When you're buying a home security system, look for UL approval on the equipment and, if your system will be monitored, for the central station. (UL standards for company operations and installation and testing apply mainly to companies that install commercial security systems, so don't expect to find this kind of certification for firms doing home installations.)

Manufacturers can submit their products to UL for evaluation. Products that have passed UL's rigorous testing are issued a registered UL listing number. The product is stamped or labeled with the UL mark. UL periodically audits the manufacturer to verify that the product is being manufactured exactly as it was originally tested and approved. To ensure that you're getting the most reliable security system, insist that all equipment be "UL Listed."

To get the UL stamp of approval, central monitoring stations must meet UL's standards for the building, equipment, and procedures. To maintain UL certification, the companies must pass an annual inspection. When you choose a monitoring service, you're counting on the reliability of that service, and UL certification is one of the assurances you can check. Ask to see a copy of the UL certificate, and check the expiration date on the certificate to ensure that it is current.

Installing a **Wireless Alarm** System

With a few hand tools and a little patience, you'll be able to install a wireless security system. The steps shown here give you an idea of what's involved in installing this kind of system, but the system you choose may be different. Always follow the manufacturer's installation instructions to ensure successful installation and trouble-free operation.

Step 1. Plan Your System

Decide where to place the main control panel inside your home. Many wireless systems combine the CPU and keypad into one unit that can be mounted on the wall or placed on a table. For ease of use, locate the control panel near your most frequently used exterior door, and near an electrical outlet that's NOT controlled by a switch. Just be sure it isn't in plain view from that door or nearby windows.

▼ *Here's a sample plan: The windows are marked in blue and exterior doors are red. (CP) is the control panel, (AS) is the alarm siren. The sensors are marked: (D) door, (M) motion, (S) smoke, (H) heat, and (W) window.*

Determine where to place the security and fire sensors. In pencil, write the location on the back of each sensor. Keep the sensors and the control panel in one location to program the system.

Pick a location for your interior alarm siren. For some systems, the siren simply plugs into an electrical outlet, communicating with the control panel over your house wiring. Choose an inconspicuous location, but don't muffle the siren by putting it behind upholstered furniture.

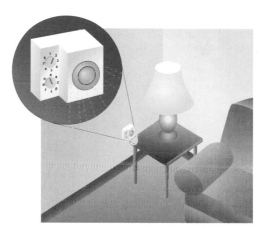

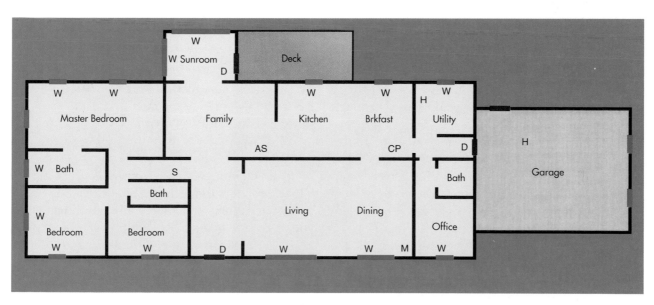

Installing a **Wireless Alarm** System

Step 2. Install the Control Panel

If you decide to mount the control panel on the wall, place it at a comfortable height. Be sure you can easily read the display and press numbers on the keypad. Have all members of the family who'll use the system do the same thing to ensure the proper height. For most folks, that's about the same height as the thermostat.

To protect the wires from being tampered with, you'll need to run a short length of wire behind the wall from the back of the control panel to just above the outlet. Most systems use two-conductor,

18-gauge wire. First, turn off the power to the outlet. Drill a small hole directly behind the control panel and another just below the outlet, then fish the wire through the wall. If you plan to have the system monitored, also route two-pair, 24-gauge telephone wire from the control panel to the junction box where your phone lines enter the house.

Following the manufacturer's instructions, connect the transformer wire to the control panel and transformer. Install the backup battery in the control panel, switch the circuit back on and plug in the transformer. For monitored systems, don't connect the phone lines just yet. Have an alarm company technician do this when he/she is there programming your control panel to communicate with the central station.

Step 3. Program and Install the Alarm Siren

Using a small screwdriver, turn the programming dials on the siren to select a "house code" that you'll program into the control panel. Plug the unit into an electrical outlet NOT controlled by a switch.

Step 4. Program the Control Panel

All of the alarm system's features are programmed into the control panel using the keypad. Some systems "talk" you through the process with a synthesized voice. Before you begin, carefully read the manufacturer's programming instructions and fill out the worksheets that came with the system.

Doing this prep work makes the installation go more smoothly and ensures the system will operate properly when you're finished.

The "identity" of a sensor is programmed into the control panel when you trip that sensor. Your penciled notes on the sensors help ensure that you'll get the sensors back to the correct locations.

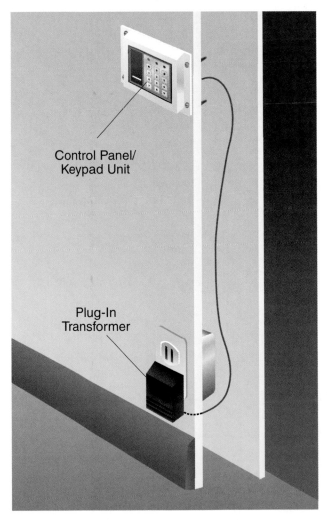

Control Panel/
Keypad Unit

Plug-In
Transformer

Step 5. Install the Sensors

The most commonly used door and window sensors have two parts: a transmitter and a magnet. Mount the transmitter to the edge of the door or window frame and the magnet to the door or window. The alignment of the two parts is critical. Be sure the alignment marks on the pieces match up correctly.

Passive Infrared Motion Sensors (PIRs), glass-break sensors, and smoke detectors install easily with a couple of screws and plastic sheetrock anchors. These devices, however, require careful placement for maximum effectiveness, so be sure to follow the guidelines in the instructions.

Step 6. Test the System

After all the components have been installed, you'll need to be sure the system works properly. Test every sensor and all the functions of the control panel. The test mode on the control panel provides audible feedback as you test each sensor.

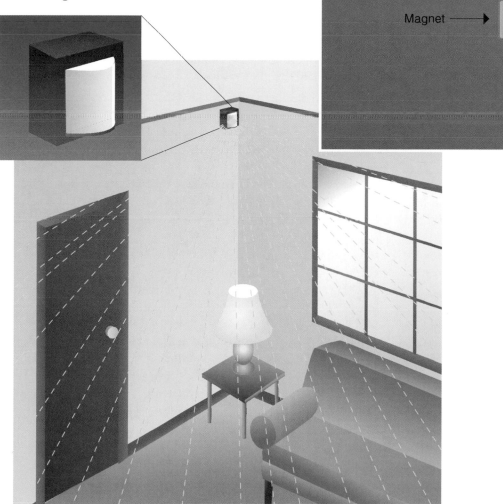

Transmitter

Magnet →

Choosing and Installing **Smoke Detectors**

Even a relatively small fire can fill a house with smoke in a matter of minutes. For this reason, many local building codes and home insurers now require smoke detectors in new houses and apartments.

Smoke detectors come in two types—photoelectric and ionization. Photoelectric types beam light into a chamber containing a photocell. When smoke enters, it scatters the light, causing part of it to contact the photocell and trigger the alarm. Slow, smoldering fires set these off more readily than fast, flaming blazes.

Ionization units use a radioactive source that ionizes or breaks up the air inside the detector and gives it a small electrical charge. Smoke particles reduce the current flow, which sounds the warning. Ionization detectors respond more quickly than photoelectric units to fast, flaming fires.

Which Works Best?

Each type has its advantages and drawbacks. Most photoelectric models run on house current, which means you get no protection in a power outage or in an electrical fire. Ionization units run on house current, batteries, or both. Besides reacting more slowly to smoldering fires, they're also more susceptible to false alarms. To increase your peace of mind, you may want to use one of each—an ionization detector in your bedroom hallway and a photocell unit in the main living area.

Truly deluxe fire protection systems also include heat sensors wired in tandem so that all alarms will sound if just one senses excessive heat or smoke. As part of a residential alarm system, these sensors are wired to the home's control panel which can send a signal to the central monitoring station in the event of a fire. Also, these systems often have their own power source and backup, eliminating any concerns about house current or needing to change batteries.

Playing With Fire

According to the National Fire Protection Association, smoking is the leading cause of fatal residential fires. Kids playing with matches and lighters runs a close second— keep them out of children's reach.
If you smoke:
☐ *Never smoke in bed or when you're feeling drowsy.*
☐ *Use only large, noncombustible ashtrays designed to keep cigarettes from falling out.*
☐ *Douse matches, butts, and ashes with water before discarding them in the trash.*

Maintaining Smoke Detectors

Test each smoke detector monthly. Most have a test button that sounds the alarm when you press it. If yours doesn't have a test button, light a candle, blow out the flame after a few seconds, then hold the smoking wick about 6 inches below the smoke detector. The smoke should trip the alarm.

Replace the batteries in battery-powered smoke detectors annually. Fire prevention specialists suggest doing this on a date you can easily remember— your birthday, for instance, or the day you set the clocks back.

While you're replacing the battery, take a moment to clean the inside of the detector and its vents with a soft brush.

If you need to replace an ionization detector, bear in mind that it contains radioactive material and you shouldn't throw it in the household trash. Instead, take it to a recycling center or send it back to the manufacturer.

Installing Smoke Detectors

Most smoke detectors take only a few minutes to install and come with complete instructions. Knowing where to locate them, though, can help you decide how many you need, and might also have a bearing on the type you select.

☐ Attach each unit to a ceiling, or high on a wall about 8 or 10 inches below ceiling level.

☐ Don't install smoke detectors in corners because air circulation there is poor.

☐ Don't install smoke detectors close to the kitchen, furnace, garage, or fireplace, or just outside a bathroom door.

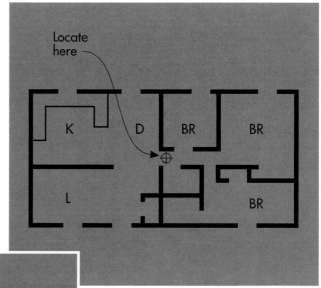

▲ *In a single-floor home with bedrooms clustered together, you can install one unit in a hallway between the bedroom and living areas.*

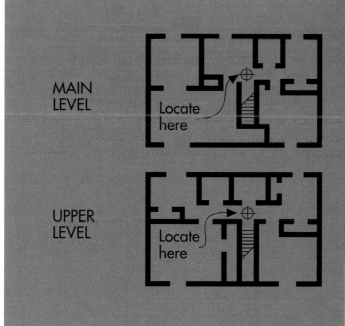

◄ *If your sleeping areas are spread out or are on different levels, you'll need at least two smoke detectors. Mount one near the stairway on each level, as shown here, and outside bedroom doors that are more than 30 feet away.*

➤ *Protect your basement. Smoke and heat rise, so install a smoke detector at the top of the basement stairway.*

Fire Extinguisher
ABCs

The right fire extinguisher, properly used, can keep a small household fire from turning into a conflagration. A fire in your home can involve any one or a combination of three things: combustible solids, flammable liquids, or live electricity. To protect your family, arm yourself with a fire extinguisher rated ABC to handle all of these types of fires.

☐ Class A fires consume combustible solids, such as paper, wood, fabric, and most plastics. Class A extinguishers expel water propelled by a gas or are easily pumped. Foam also puts out Class A fires.

☐ Class B fires are those that burn in flammable liquids, such as grease, oil, gasoline, and kerosene. Foam, dry chemical, and carbon dioxide (CO_2) all work against liquid fires; don't use water because it will spread the flames.

☐ Class C fires are caused by live electricity. With the power off, these become Class A or Class B fires. Use a CO_2 or dry chemical extinguisher on electrical fires. Never use foam or water, because you could suffer a serious shock and/or spread the fire.

Shopping Tips

Insist that any fire extinguisher you buy be rated by an independent testing agency such as Underwriters Laboratory (UL). Also, look closely at the label for a number that indicates the capacity of its contents. The larger the number, the greater the capacity, but also the more the extinguisher will weigh. (Home fire extinguishers typically weigh from 10 to 36 pounds.)

Think, too, about how many extinguishers you will need. At minimum, buy one each for the kitchen, basement, and garage. You might want to provide a fourth for a bedroom area.

As soon as you get the extinguisher home, read the directions in front of the whole family. Recheck the extinguishers monthly to make sure they're fully charged.

Mount each fire extinguisher near a doorway, no more than 5 feet above the floor and as far as possible from any location in which a fire could likely break out, such as a range, fireplace, or wood stove.

1 *Have someone call the fire department immediately, and alert others to evacuate the house. Remove extinguisher from its mounting, set it on the floor or a countertop and pull the lock pin as shown.*

2 *Stand at least 6 feet from the flames, with your back to a doorway so you can make a speedy exit, if necessary. Hold the extinguisher upright in both hands and aim its nozzle at the base of the flames.*

3 *Squeeze the levers of the release handle together and sweep the stream side to side across the base of the flames. Spray until flames are extinguished, then watch to see if they rekindle. Be prepared to spray again.*

Hot Tip

After the fire is out or you've emptied the extinguisher, leave the house and wait for fire fighters to arrive. They'll check to make sure flames won't reignite. Remember to have the fire extinguisher recharged or to buy a new one.

Electrical
Safety

Electricity poses a double threat to home safety: It can cause a painful, even deadly shock, and it can set a house on fire. Check out your home's wiring against this list of electrical problems.

☐ Fuses or circuit breakers that frequently blow are sure signs that a circuit is dangerously overloaded. Do not substitute a larger capacity fuse. Reduce the load to the circuit or have an electrician upgrade your home wiring

☐ A tangle of extension cords is another sign that your home is under-wired. Try to avoid extension cords. If you must use one, make sure it's rated for the appliance plugged into the cord. Never run extension cords under rugs, over hooks, or through door openings where the insulation could fray.

☐ Frayed cords and cracked plugs should be wrapped with electrical tape or, better yet, replaced. Never use any electrical device with a defective cord or plug.

☐ Ungrounded receptacles, the old-fashioned two-slot kind, lack protection against electrical shock. Upgrading receptacles may be as simple as replacing them, as shown on page 55. But first have an electrician determine if your home's system is grounded. Installing grounded receptacles in an ungrounded system provides a false sense of security and is a violation of building codes.

☐ A switch or receptacle that sparks when you use it is defective and needs to be replaced, as shown on pages 54-55. The same goes for receptacles that don't grip plugs firmly.

☐ No Ground-Fault Circuit Interrupter (GFCI) protection: this device instantly shuts off the power if you happen to come in contact with a live wire or an appliance while touching plumbing components or standing on wet earth. Most codes require GFCI protection for all bathroom and outdoor receptacles, and some also specify GFCI devices for any kitchen receptacle within 6 feet of a sink.

Choosing GFCI Devices

Fuses and circuit breakers protect the wiring in your home. A GFCI protects people who might otherwise get a dangerous shock.

In a GFCI, a microprocessor senses tiny leakages of current and shuts off the power instantly. In most circumstances, leaking current isn't a big problem. In a properly grounded system, most of it is carried back to the service panel. What remains would scarcely give you a tickle. But if you happen to be well-grounded—standing on a wet lawn, for instance, or turning on a faulty hair dryer while the other hand is shutting off a faucet—that tiny bit of current would pass through your body on its way to the earth. As little as ⅓ amp, just about enough to light a 25-watt bulb, can be dangerous.

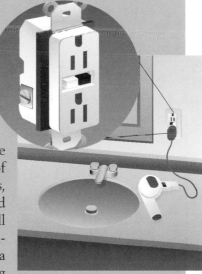

GFCI protection is a good idea anywhere you might be in contact with water while using electricity. As shown here, there are three types of GFCIs: plug-ins, receptacles, and breakers. To install a plug-in unit, simply insert it into a receptacle and plug in the appliance. A GFCI receptacle replaces a conventional receptacle, and a GFCI breaker protects every outlet on the circuit; it's best installed by an electrician.

Replacing
Switches and Receptacles

Replacing a Switch

Most of today's switches can be wired in one of two ways: by pushing bare wires into holes in the back of the device or by wrapping the wires around screw terminals on one or both sides. Electricians believe the screw terminals provide a more secure connection and many wrap electrical tape around the switch body for added safety.

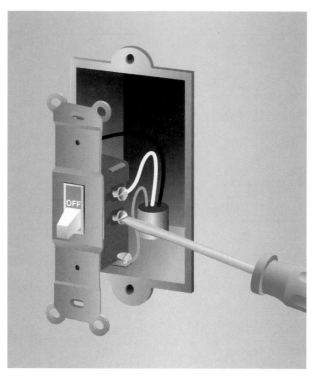

1 *Turn off power to the circuit, remove the cover plate, remove the screws holding the switch to the box, and gently pull out the switch. Loosen the screw terminals or push a nail into the wire-release holes and disconnect the wires.*

2 *Inspect the wires in the box and wrap any damaged insulation with electrical tape. Attach the wires to the terminals of the new switch and wrap electrical tape around the body of the switch, so the terminals are covered.*

3 *Carefully fold the wires back into the box and fasten the switch to the box with the mounting screws. Don't force anything; switches can break and short out from the pressure exerted by forced wiring.*

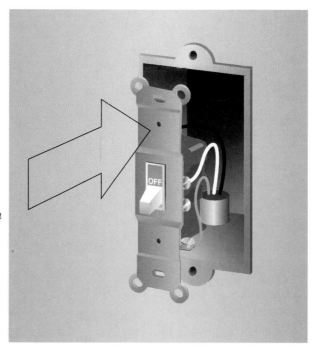

Replacing a Receptacle

As with switches, you can wire receptacles through holes in the back or screw terminals on the sides. The screw terminals hold better.

1 *Shut off power to the box. Note which wires are attached to which terminals (make notations on tape attached to the wires). Loosen the terminal screws or push a nail into the wire-release holes and disconnect the wires.*

2 *Inspect the wires in the box and wrap electrical tape around any damaged insulation. Attach the wires to the terminals, positioning each wire so it hooks clockwise on the terminal screws. Firmly tighten the terminal screws.*

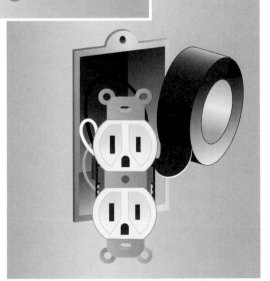

3 *Wrap the body of the receptacle with electrical tape, covering all the terminals. Carefully tuck the wires and the receptacle back into the box, and fasten the receptacle to the box with the mounting screws. Don't force the receptacle; it could crack.*

Strategies for Safety And Security

Being safe and secure in and around your home is a lifestyle.

Everyone makes choices—sometimes several—that significantly affect the safety and security of their families and their homes. Some of the decisions that don't seem like choices at the time are actually negative choices—choosing not to lock the door or close the windows when you go to the store, for example, or not buying a fire extinguisher. You can fail to perform such actions many times with no serious repercussions. It's the one time something happens to you, a family member, or a close friend that can make you regret your choice. You have to make conscious decisions to keep accidents or theft from affecting you directly.

A safe and secure lifestyle doesn't require overwhelming changes. It is, for the most part, a matter of awareness and common sense. Besides, it's easy to incorporate many of the changes into your daily routine. It may take you a while to review everything, but the old maxim, "better safe than sorry," is a reminder that it's time well spent.

Kid Stuff

Children in single-parent and two-income families are often home alone in the hours after school. Protect your youngsters by teaching them these safety and security ABCs.

☐ *Make sure they know their full names, addresses (including city and state), and phone numbers (with area code). They should also memorize parents' work phone numbers.*

☐ *Be sure they know to call 911 or "O" in emergencies. Practice making emergency calls with a toy phone.*

☐ *Explain how to give directions to your home in an emergency.*

☐ *Tell them never to accept rides or gifts from someone they and you don't know well. Children should know to stay at least 8 feet away from a stranger in a car who stops to ask for directions or anything else.*

☐ *Teach older kids how to use your home's door and window locks—and the alarm system, if you have one.*

☐ *If no one will be home when your children get there, have them check in with you or a neighbor as soon as they arrive home. Post numbers by each telephone.*

☐ *Provide them with a house key that they can put in a safe place, such as inside a pocket or sock. Don't leave a key under the mat or hang it in plain view on a string around a child's neck.*

☐ *Insist that they never let anyone into your home, including other kids, without your permission.*

☐ *Tell them to never let a caller at the door or on the phone know that they're alone. Tell them to say "Mom can't come to the phone (or door) right now."*

☐ *Set a good example with your own actions—lock the doors and windows and find out who's at the door before opening it.*

☐ *Make sure they know how to escape in case of fire or another emergency.*

☐ *Explain that they should not go in the house or apartment without you if things don't look right—if the door is open or a screen is ripped.*

☐ *Listen carefully to your children's fears, and their feelings about people or places that scare them or make them feel uneasy. Tell them to trust their instincts.*

Get in the **Habit of Security**

The best locks, lighting, and alarms that money can buy won't protect your home if you don't use them conscientiously. Like buckling your car's seat belt or looking both ways before you cross a street, effective home security depends on developing habits that become second nature for each member of your family.

Know Your Neighbors

Crime prevention specialists wholeheartedly agree that a tightly knit neighborhood—neighbors looking out for each other—is the single greatest deterrent to crimes against people and property. Elderly neighbors home during the day, night owls, moms keeping an eye on the neighborhood children, even the kids themselves, notice something amiss.

When something threatens the peace or makes you suspicious, you needn't take any personal risks. Instead, simply pick up the phone and call 911, and then decide whether or not you should notify other neighbors.

Of course, to do this effectively, you need to be acquainted with your neighbors, and they with you. Knowing each others' work schedules, home and business phone numbers, children's names, and the vehicles most often in the area can help everyone spot a crime in progress—or about to happen—and maybe enable police to catch a miscreant in the act.

Protecting Off-Site Property

Not all your "stuff" is necessarily under your roof. Important papers in a safe-deposit box at the bank, or extra furniture at a mini-storage facility still needs to be protected.

☐ **Check your insurance policy.**
Your homeowner's insurance policy may not cover all items stored off-site. And expensive items, such as jewelry, may need a rider, just as if you kept the items at home.

☐ **Keep an inventory.**
Should something happen, you'll need to verify what you stored and its value. This helps both the police in identifying your items and the insurance company in completing your claim.

☐ **Ask about the business' insurance.**
The bank or mini-storage facility may only be insured for losses to their property—the boxes or buildings—and you must insure the contents.

☐ **Check in from time to time.**
Don't assume that because you locked something up safe and sound it's going to stay that way. Banks take precautions to ensure no one else gets in your safe-deposit box, but that doesn't mean it absolutely can't happen.

Items in mini-storage are more vulnerable. Access to the storage area often isn't very restricted. If the walls between spaces aren't reinforced, a thief can break the least-sturdy lock and get to an entire row.

Neighborhood Crime-Stoppers

You can promote old-fashioned neighborliness informally, or you and your neighbors can sponsor a formal organization with the help of your local police or sheriff's department. They'll send a crime prevention officer to meet with your group, offer tips on home and neighborhood security, tell you how to best protect yourselves, and how to help police capture suspects. Best of all, they'll put up signs that show your neighborhood group is on the lookout for crime—signs that will warn prowlers to move on.

What's involved? As with any community endeavor, you'll need to attend a few meetings, learn about crime prevention, and share the information with your neighbors. You also may be asked to help out with copying and distributing materials, making phone calls, organizing meetings, or providing refreshments. Some neighborhood crime prevention groups ask for a few dollars in dues from members; others rely on voluntary contributions. In either case, each member's main duty is to serve as the neighborhood's eyes and ears.

Identify Your Belongings

Marking your valuables with an identifying name or number that can be traced back to you serves two purposes: It tells a thief that the items will be difficult or even impossible to fence; and if the property is recovered, police can return it to you.

According to police estimates, if people marked their property, the amount recovered would double—and so would the number of arrests for theft.

You can identify your belongings in one of two ways—with a pen that has ink visible only under ultraviolet light, and with an engraver you can check out from your police department.

The pens, which cost about $5, let you mark items as soon as you buy them, but the mark can't be seen; engraving makes an obvious mark that might deter some burglars. Some police departments also supply window decals that can discourage would-be thieves from breaking into your home in the first place.

While you're marking your property, make a thorough inventory of it, as explained on pages 68-71. The serial numbers from an inventory can aid police and make it easier to prove a loss to your insurance company.

Get in the **Habit of Security**

When Your Name Is In the News

When a family member, relative, or neighbor passes away, arrange to have someone guard their house during the funeral. Some thieves read obituaries carefully, though you won't see them at the church.

The same goes for wedding announcements, awards ceremonies, and any other publicity that includes your address and the time of an event that will leave your home vulnerable.

Scam artists often read obituaries, too. Then they show up at the bereaved's door a few days later with an expensive bible, jewelry, or some other item that they claim the deceased person made a down payment on. These swindlers are often very skilled at manipulating victims and taking advantage of a very emotional situation.

When You Sell Your Home

Opening your home to prospective buyers also opens it up to prospecting thieves and even attackers. Here are safety precautions you and your real estate agent should follow.

☐ Check all doors and windows after showing your home. A would-be intruder could unlock one and return later.

☐ Require that every interested buyer have an agent with him or her. Never let in someone who stops by unannounced. Instead, refer them to your agent.

☐ Ask agents to leave business cards when they show your home.

☐ Never leave valuables—such as money, jewelry, or credit cards—lying around when the house is open.

☐ If you're selling your own home, ask for identification from potential homebuyers or take a picture of each visitor.

☐ Always have another adult there when you show your home.

If You've Been Robbed

You return home and, with a sinking feeling, discover a forced door or other sign of illegal entry. What should you do?

☐ ***Call 911.*** *Do not enter the premises. Instead, call the police from a neighbor's house or use a cell phone. The intruder could still be inside, and a burglary could turn into a violent confrontation.*

☐ ***Wait*** *for the police to arrive. Don't walk around the house, because you could destroy evidence that might assist them. Let the police check inside your home first, then walk through it with them.*

☐ ***Report*** *everything that's obviously missing right away. You'll need to make a more detailed search later, but you can always amend a missing property report.*

☐ ***Resecure*** *your home. If entry was through a door or window, board it up with plywood until you can make a permanent repair. Intruders sometimes return to the scenes of their crimes for stuff they couldn't carry out the first time around.*

☐ ***Notify*** *your insurance agent within 24 hours. He or she will need an itemized list of what's missing. (For help in preparing one, see property inventory on pages 68-71.)*

Note: Only rarely does stolen property get back to its rightful owner, even when the thief who took it is caught. Burglars are as speedy at disposing of ill-gotten gains as they are at stealing them in the first place.

Vacation Checklist

You've planned an itinerary, made reservations, and now you're about to take off on that much-anticipated vacation. But before you start packing, take these steps to secure your home and belongings while you're away.

□ Stop mail, newspapers, and other deliveries. Or, ask a neighbor to bring them inside every day. A pile of stuff on your front porch tells a passerby that, although lights may be on, nobody's home.

□ Arrange to have yard work done. Unmowed grass, unshoveled snow, and unraked leaves also give away a home's unoccupied status.

□ Have a neighbor set out trash on normal collection days. And have empty cans and recycle bins removed the same day.

□ Tell a neighbor or whomever is watching the house where you can be reached if there's an emergency. Offer to reciprocate when they're gone.

□ If you have an alarm system, make sure that it's in working order. If it's connected to a monitoring service, tell them when you'll be gone and where you're going, along with a phone number of the person keeping an eye on things.

□ Check timers. Set and use them for a day or two before leaving to be sure they turn lights and a radio or TV on and off at appropriate times.

□ Turn the ringers on phones down or off. A phone that rings and rings tells a prowler there's no one there to pick it up.

□ Don't change the outgoing message on your answering machine. Never program it to announce that you're out of town or to give another number where you can be reached. Instead, call in periodically and retrieve any messages.

□ Avoid discussing your travel plans in public places. A stranger could overhear them, follow you home, and return after you've left.

□ Use luggage tags that can't be easily read. Someone standing behind you at the airport check-in counter could note your address. Or, use your business address on your luggage tags.

□ If you leave a car at home, park it in the driveway, not in the garage, and arrange to have it moved from time to time, or have a neighbor park in your drive.

□ Unplug the electric garage door opener. (For more about garage security, see pages 26-27.)

□ In the summer, set the air conditioning to a higher temperature, but don't turn it off. A silent compressor on a blazing hot day is a good indication that the house is unoccupied.

□ Leave blinds and shades in their normal position. Windows that remain covered day and night can attract unwanted attention.

□ The best choice is to hire a house-sitter you can trust. The sitter can perform the jobs listed above for the neighbors and tend to plants and pets.

□ Take one last walk-around. After everyone is in the car, check to make sure that all windows and doors are securely locked and that the alarm system has been properly armed.

When You're
Home

Many intruders steer clear of occupied houses, but that doesn't mean you should assume nothing can happen. A break-in when you're there could put family members at risk. Here are eight key at-home security habits well worth cultivating.

☐ **Use the locks.** Get in the a habit of keeping doors and windows locked—even when you're home. Don't leave the front door unlocked when you're working in the backyard or vice-versa. Encourage children to lock up, too.

☐ **Keep the keys.** Know the whereabouts of all keys to the house. Don't hide an extra key under the doormat, in the mail box, in a flower pot, or any place else. Separate the house keys from the car keys so a parking lot attendant can't make a copy of your house key—and never attach an address tag to your key ring. (See "Key Concepts" on page 23 for more on keeping track of keys.)

☐ **Screen every unknown person who comes to the door.** Before you open the door, ask to see photo identification of anyone you don't recognize—even if the person is wearing a uniform or is driving a commercial truck; both could be fake or stolen. As an added measure of protection, call the company and verify that the person works there and has been dispatched to your house.

Never admit a stranger who wants to make a phone call. Instead, offer to make the call for them. If a stranger says he or she has been injured, offer to call 911, but don't open the door.

Anyone selling door to door should receive the same scrutiny. Pass items back and forth through a slightly opened screen door rather than inviting them in; install a chain on your screen door to ensure it won't open any more than you want it to. And don't walk away from the unlocked door while they're still standing there.

☐ **Vary your routine.** If neighbors can set their watches by your comings and goings, a potential intruder can figure out when you'll be gone, and for how long. There's not much you can do about the hours you're at work, but going to the grocery store, for example, or the health club at different times of day can make your habits less predictable.

☐ **Use the phone wisely.** Avoid giving information to telephone callers you don't know, or even ones who claim to be friends of family members or representatives of a company you know. Never record a message on your answering machine that announces no one is home. Instead, say "We're not available to take your call right now."

If you are home alone, make that less obvious to callers by talking to someone else. Answering the phone by saying, "I've got it" into thin air just before you say hello into the phone may seem silly, but it

▲ *Keeping a computer at hand but not in plain view of a window can be tricky. These tall, uncovered windows are well above ground level and blocked by trees. So putting the computer to the side of the windows makes it almost unnoticeable from the outside.*

□ **Keep valuables out of sight.** If a window peeper sees a purse, wallet, jewelry, or cell phone laying in plain sight, he may be tempted to "smash-and-grab"—simply smash the window and grab items within easy reach. Keep this in mind when placing items within your home, too. A computer, television, or stereo system situated directly in front of a window may make the "pickings" easy. And if you place them across from a window, you give anyone passing by an idea of what you own.

Garages and sheds left open are prime viewing for a thief. Lightweight lawn mowers, snow blowers, and bikes are prime targets.

□ **Track your trash.** If you've just treated the family to a new stereo, television set, or computer, don't set the empty boxes out on trash day in plain view of passersby. Instead, break down the boxes and put them in trash bags.

Also, be aware that rifling through household trash to get identification information has become fairly common. Armed with credit-card numbers, ATM receipts, bank statements, or unopened loan and credit card offers, criminals can turn your trash into easy money and create a major headache for you. Consider purchasing an inexpensive paper shredder to make your paper trash unreadable.

gives the caller the impression that someone else is there with you.

New phone services can help keep nuisance calls from ringing on your phone. For example, you can set your phone to block anonymous calls and keep anyone who doesn't want themselves identified from getting through on your line.

To make sure you can get to a phone when you need one, put phones in several rooms. If you live alone, consider tucking one in the master bedroom closet. If you hear or see something that troubles you, you can duck into the closet to call the police to have it checked out.

□ **Be alert when you're out and about.** Taking an early-morning run or walking the dog shouldn't put you on high alert, but you should always be aware of your surroundings, even in your own neighborhood. Get into the habit of simply looking around every time you enter or exit your home or get in or out of your car.

Security experts recommend *not* wearing headphones while you exercise in public—walking or jogging, for example, or even working in the backyard. You can't hear someone coming, and headphones are a clear indication that you're not tuned into what's going on around you.

Security for **Apartment** and **Condominium** Dwellers

Security in an apartment building or complex rests largely in the hands of your landlord or condominium association, but common-sense precautions on your part also can make a big difference.

☐ Since you can't do much in the way of improvements, your best option is to evaluate an apartment for security before you sign the lease.

☐ Start at the front door—check the lock on the door to the building. And, make sure the door to your apartment has at least two locks—one should be a dead bolt—and a good chain.

☐ When you move in, insist that the locks be changed. (Swapping the cylinder with one from another vacant unit costs nothing and takes just a few minutes.) If you don't like what's provided, consider adding a surface-mounted deadbolt lock (see page 24). Be sure to get management approval before you install it, or ask that they do it for you.

☐ A solid-core door is just as essential on an apartment as it is on a house. Ask to have one installed if the existing door is hollow-core. Many newer apartments have solid-core doors for fire safety.

☐ Never open the door of your unit to a stranger. Most communities have building codes that require peephole viewers in apartment doors; get in the habit of using yours.

☐ Check the windows, especially sliding glass doors that open to the balcony. Even on an upper floor in a high rise, a daring burglar can gain access, especially if balconies are close to each other. (To learn about securing windows and sliding doors, see pages 32-33.)

☐ For additional security, invest in portable door and window alarms or a wireless system that you can take with you when you move out.

☐ Never leave the door to your apartment unlocked, whether you're home or not.

☐ Check the security of the building's public areas. Look for adequate lighting in the parking lot, in hallways, and in the laundry room and storage areas. Make sure the emergency phone in the elevator works.

☐ If your building has an intercom system, make sure it works. Never buzz in someone you don't know. Instead, refer them to the manager.

☐ Don't put your first name or initial on your mailbox or apartment door; strangers don't need to know your gender or to assume only one adult is living there.

☐ Think about safety, too. Be sure your apartment has working smoke detectors, and that public areas have smoke detectors, too.

☐ Know the best way to get out of your building in case of a fire.

Security in the Country

Crime doesn't happen just in urban areas; folks who live in the country have just as much need to secure their homes and property as anyone, perhaps more. The remoteness of a country home can make it even more attractive to criminals—both those who want to take things, and those who want to get rid of things.

☐ *Know your property and check it regularly. That bog out of sight of the house may be useless to you but seen as a perfect dumping ground by someone else.*

☐ *Maintain fences, gates, and locks. Get in the habit of closing and locking gates, and locking buildings.*

☐ *Install adequate lighting at the street, along the drive, and around the house and buildings. To conserve electricity and ensure the lights are on when needed, use timers or motion sensors.*

☐ *Tools and equipment stored in outbuildings or on the far corners of a large property can attract thieves. Check outbuildings regularly.*

☐ *Install "eyes and ears" to alert you to someone coming onto your property. Electronic "eyes" at the end of the drive let you know when a car pulls in, and the "ears" of an intercom let you talk to someone at the gate or at the door.*

Securing Special
Targets

Cash, silverware, jewelry, stamp and coin collections, firearms, furs, camera equipment—thieves love valuables like these because they are easy to carry and easy to fence. They know where to look for them, too, so don't assume that items concealed in dresser drawers or under the mattress will escape their attention.

The most secure place for precious possessions is a safe-deposit box, where there's almost no chance they'll be stolen or destroyed by fire. But a safe-deposit box doesn't hold much, and accessibility is limited to banking hours. Here are other ways to provide extra protection for your special property.

Home Safes

Before you go shopping for a home safe, consider what you want it to do. Good safes carry Underwriters Laboratories (UL) ratings. Fire-resistant safes include fireclay insulation that will protect paper documents up to 1 hour at 1,700 degrees F (Class C), up to 2 hours at 1,850 degrees F (Class B), and up to 4 hours at 2,000 degrees F (Class A). A Class B or C safe should adequately protect irreplaceable papers. You can also buy specialized safes that protect computer tapes and disks from data loss.

To protect against damage from a collapsing building, these units also must pass tough explosion and impact

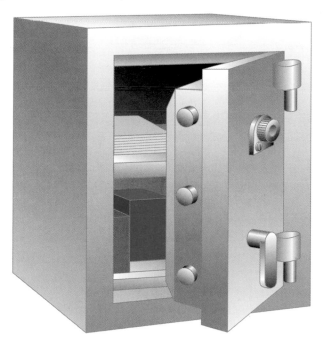

tests. A fire-resistant safe costs less than any other. Keep irreplaceable papers in this one.

Money chests, secured to your home's structure, generally are smaller in size and higher in price. These are UL-rated, also, based on their ability to withstand attacks with tools (TL), torches (TR), and explosives (TX). Many, but not all, home safes are rated as TL. On those that are, the TL rating carries a number that indicates how many minutes the safe can resist an attack by an expert who knows what he's doing. A TL-15 safe, for example, will withstand 15 minutes of continuous drilling.

Money chests, though not always lightweight, can be pried out of a frame wall or floor, carried off, and cracked by the thief later. That's why money chests are best installed in a masonry wall or floor, or soundly bolted to framing.

Combination safes (see picture below) consist of a burglar-resistant money chest inside a fire-resistant safe. These units have thick steel walls, an even thicker door, and a combination lock with a relocking device. This ensures that if a lock is attacked with tools, it will lock permanently until it is drilled out. A combination safe can be bolted to the floor to prevent the entire safe from being taken. Best of all is a safe that is set in concrete in a foundation wall.

Securing Special
Targets

Jewelry

What's the room in a home that burglars usually head for first? According to police, the master bedroom. That's because bedrooms usually contain the items thieves are looking for—firearms, cash, and, especially, jewelry.

Heirloom jewelry belongs in a safe-deposit box or very sturdy safe. You might decide to hide other jewelry in a safe (see page 65) or the basement. (That's typically the last place thieves search, though they may pass through on the way upstairs.)

Another strategy that could protect your most treasured jewelry is to use a decoy. Leave a box of costume jewelry in plain view; a thief might grab it and not bother to look for the expensive items.

Also, never leave jewelry lying around in plain sight where a maid, repair person, or other outsider might spot it. Sometimes even honest people can be sorely tempted.

Bicycles

To ensure that a thief doesn't speed off on your ten-speed, lock it up at home as securely as you would in a public place. Also, register all family bicycles with your local police. Engraving your state's two-letter abbreviation, followed by your name or a number on record with the police, can help in recovering the bike if it's stolen.

Firearms

Gun collections pose a double threat: They're attractive to thieves and also to curious children—too often with tragic consequences. Store firearms unloaded, and keep ammunition locked up in a separate place. For safety's sake, secure each weapon with a trigger lock.

Display cases are the worst places to stow firearms. They attract attention and are easy to break into. Don't hide guns in a bedroom closet, either. That's one of the first places burglars look. Instead, consider buying a steel security gun cabinet equipped with anti-drill locks. Bolt the cabinet to wall studs or, better yet, encase it in a masonry wall.

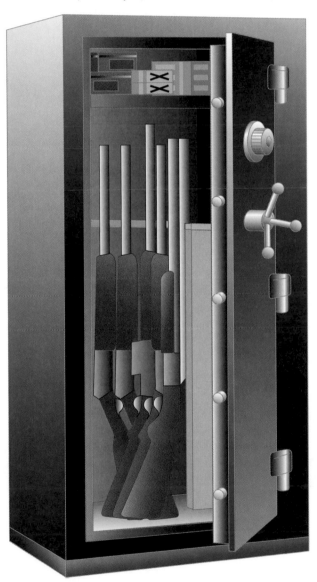

Converting a Standard Closet Into a **Security Closet**

Security Closets

No closet offers the security of a burglar- or fire-resistant safe. However, you can beef one up to protect valuables against grab-it-and-run thieves who commit most household break-ins.

Begin by lining the interior with ½-inch plywood or particleboard. It's easy to cut or even kick a hole in ordinary drywall. Treat your "safe" closet's door as if it were a point of entry to your home. Use a metal-clad solid-core door. Make sure it's carefully fitted into a sturdy frame. A third hinge in the center adds resistance to prying on that side. Because most closet doors swing outward, you'll want to secure them with metal door pins, as explained on page 20. If the door swings inward, fasten the door stops to the frame with the longest screws possible.

On the latch side, install a strong dead-bolt lock (page 25). Protect the door from being pried open by installing a heavy metal strip along the latch edge, as shown.

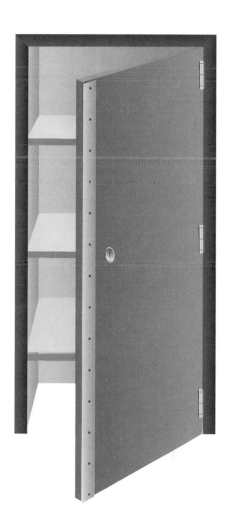

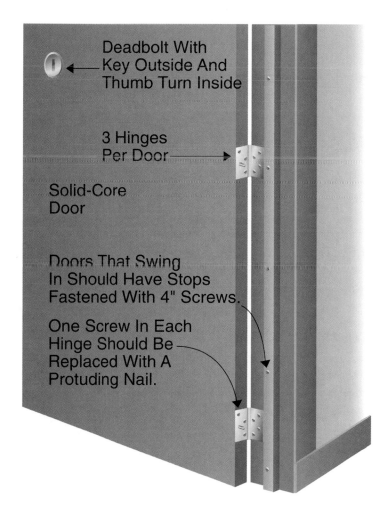

Deadbolt With Key Outside And Thumb Turn Inside

3 Hinges Per Door

Solid-Core Door

Doors That Swing In Should Have Stops Fastened With 4" Screws.

One Screw In Each Hinge Should Be Replaced With A Protuding Nail.

Home
Inventory

How will you know what's been lost if you don't know what you have?

Your blessings are the first thing to count when disaster strikes and no one is hurt. The next tally is your losses. Whether burglary, natural events, or fire caused the disaster, some or all of your household possessions are gone and need to be replaced.

Without a complete home inventory, however, you'll probably never know for sure everything you had and what it is worth. That means your police report and/or insurance claim will be incomplete, and chances are you won't be reimbursed for everything you lost. And remember, without the inventory, you'll be trying to construct the list right after disaster has struck—not a time when you're likely to remember each of your possessions.

That's a pretty sobering thought, but if you need a little more convincing to do a home inventory, try this exercise: Take pen and paper into the kitchen. Now, write down everything in the living room—but don't leave the kitchen! When you've finished your list, go into the living room and compare your list to what's really there. You'll be surprised by how many items you've missed. If that happened when you filled out your insurance claim form, you wouldn't receive compensation for many of the items you missed. Then try to date and value every item. Be specific: How old is the TV? How many CDs do you own? Without this information, you can't be sure an insurance claim will cover the full value of your itemized losses.

There's no time like the present to do a home inventory. The editors of *Better Homes and Gardens Family Money* magazine offer these tips:

☐ Do it now. Set a deadline for completing the task, but start now. You don't get a warning that you'll need this inventory.

☐ Note everything. If disaster strikes, you'll be replacing everything from the TV to the pots and pans, and they cost plenty to replace all at once.

☐ List everything in closets and drawers. It may not occur to you but the cost of replacing clothing and shoes adds up, too.

☐ Keep a list of items stored elsewhere—mini-storage, your in-law's garage, and safe-deposit boxes.

☐ Receipts or copies of receipts for big-ticket items—TVs, stereo equipment, computers, and other office equipment—should be kept with the inventory. Also, keep photocopies of important documents (tax returns, house title and deed, birth certificates, a list of credit card and bank account numbers) with the inventory.

☐ Collections of any value—art, antiques, Beanie Babies, or whatever else—should have a special inventory with photos, receipts, and current appraisals. And, be sure your homeowner's insurance policy covers these special items, too.

☐ Store a copy of the inventory off-site, perhaps at work or in a safe-deposit box. Also, send a copy to a trusted friend or relative who lives out of state.

This needn't become an overwhelming task. *Family Money* recommends a "quick-start" program with a detailed follow-up: Take a camera or video recorder from room to room and around the outside of your home, getting a picture of all your possessions. Put the tape or photos in your safe deposit box, then do the paperwork for the details.

Home
Inventory

Four Options

Taking an inventory is an inflexible necessity, but you get to be flexible in *how* you do it. Here are *Family Money*'s evaluations of four key choices:

☐ Written Inventory

Cost: Up to $10
Advantages: It can be simple or highly-detailed.
Tips: Take a pad of paper and walk through each room of the house. Note each item with price or appraisal, and when and where you bought it.

Organize the process by using a fill-in-the-blank inventory booklet. Your insurance company may give you one for free, or you can buy one at the bookstore.

☐ Software

Cost: $30-$70
Advantages: Easy to update.
Tips: Several household organizing programs include home inventory fill-in-the-blank forms.

Some programs allow you to export data to personal finance programs. And, some can calculate current and replacement values for items.

☐ Videotape

Cost: About $3 for the videotape, $75 to rent the videocamera, or $170 to hire a video service for two hours.
Advantages: This fast-and-fun way of documenting your possessions also documents your lifestyle.

▲ *As long as your belongings are out of closets and drawers why not do a home inventory when you move? Just take a clip board with a notepad into each room and jot down the contents of boxes as you unpack.*

Tips: Make a running narration as you tape, noting prices, and when and where items were purchased.

Record the details of your home, too: trimwork, hardware, fixtures, and furnishings. Get receipts for the big-ticket items you've shot on tape. And include a shot of a current newspaper to date the tape.

☐ Snapshots

Cost: About $5 per roll for film; $8 or less per roll for developing.
Advantages: You can capture small details, and this method also captures your lifestyle.
Tips: Take pictures of the details around your home: trimwork, hardware, fixtures, and furnishings. Photograph identifying marks such as brand names,

and include the receipt in the photo next to the big-ticket items.

What to Record

Regardless of the method or combination of methods you use to create a home inventory, you need to get *everything* on the list. Be systematic in your approach. Go room by room and note everything. If just the thought of this project seems overwhelming, start slowly.

Use this list of common household items to collect information about what you possess. In reviewing the list, you'll probably be surprised about how much you own. Store the completed inventory in a fireproof safe in your home or, better yet, in a safe-deposit box at your bank. Keep an extra copy at home and try to update the inventory every year or so.

Suggested inventory list

Kitchen	Living Room	Dining Room	Bathroom
Furniture	Sofas	Table	Electrical appliances:
Curtains	Chairs	Chairs	Hair dryer, curling
Cabinets	Carpet/Rugs	Carpet/Rugs	irons, electric razor
Lighting fixtures	Window coverings	Window coverings	Linens
Pots/Pans	Tables	China cabinet	Hamper
Utensils	Desk	Buffet	Curtains
Cutlery	Artwork	China/Flatware	
Dishes	Books	Artwork	**Garage, Basement,**
Flatware	Electronics (include		**and Attic**
Refrigerator	serial numbers):	**Bedrooms**	Furniture
Stove	Television	Furniture	Luggage
Microwave	VCR	Carpet/Rugs	Toys and games
Freezer	Stereo system	Jewelry	Lawn mower
Washer	Computer	Window coverings	Snow blower
Dryer	Telephone	Clothing	Garden tools
Small appliances:	Tapes	Electronics:	Ladders
Toaster	CDs or records	Television	Freezer
Food processor	Lamps/Fixtures	Clock radio	Camping and sports
Hand-mixer		Exercise equipment	equipment
Clock		Lighting fixtures	Tools
Food		Artwork	Shop and yard
		Books/toys	equipment
		Linens	Bikes

Parts of this inventory courtesy of the Insurance Information Institute

Homeowner's
Insurance

Should burglary or disaster damage your home and property, there are three words you don't want to hear: "That's not covered." If your homeowner's insurance policy is inadequate, you could hear that phrase a lot when you least want to.

On the face of it, buying homeowner's insurance seems a simple matter: Get enough coverage to replace what could be lost or stolen, to rebuild damaged portions of the house, and to protect yourself if someone is hurt while on your property.

That's probably why everything the insurance agent told you when you bought the policy seemed so obvious: If a tree falls on the house, the insurance, minus the deductible, will pay for it. If the mail delivery person slips on the sidewalk, it's covered. Take those scenes to the next level, however, and things get a little fuzzier. What if the tree was felled by ice? Some policies wouldn't cover the damage.

Know Your HO Numbers

The basic insurance policy for home and property is designated by the term HO, obviously enough, for "homeowner," followed by a number. The original industry standard, HO-1, only covered damage from 11 specific causes, such as fire, lightning, riot, theft, vandalism, and volcanic eruption. The limited nature of the coverage made this a less-than-popular option for most people, and this type of policy is being phased out in some states.

One step up the chain is HO-2, which covers against damage from 17 named perils. The additional items include damage caused by snow and ice, and burst pipes and water damage from freezing of the plumbing system. The increased coverage increases the cost, but you'll find it's well worth it.

A big change comes with HO-3. Rather than covering specific causes and events, everything except specific perils are covered. Floods are generally not included but you can get separate flood

insurance through the federal government. Exactly what is not covered will be stated in your policy and varies from company to company. While the cost is higher than HO-1, you're more likely to be covered when something happens.

HO-4 and HO-6 cover only property—not the structure—and most include some liability coverage. These policies are designed for renters and condo owners.

If you have a home that has historical significance, is located on a floodplain, or has any other special circumstances, talk to an independent insurance agent about coverage.

How Much Insurance?

Most newer homeowner's insurance policies are issued for 100 percent of the cost of rebuilding. The old standard, before 1990, was 80 percent, based on the assumption that some portion of your house would survive most perils, so why pay extra to insure against complete destruction? If your policy was issued before 1990, you may want to review and upgrade your coverage to the new standard.

Another rude surprise you want to avoid is making the assumption that you're 100 percent covered for the loss of your home and its contents. First, you'll need to define "100 percent." There's 100 percent of the current value. It's pretty safe to say that not everything in your house is new. So your 5-year-old television works fine, but because it's that old, it's not worth as much as it would cost you to buy a new one. If your homeowner's insurance coverage is for cash value of the contents, you'll only receive reimbursement equal to the value of your TV on the date it's stolen or destroyed.

Then there's 100 percent of what it would cost you to replace everything. Although more expensive, replacement value policies provide better coverage. The key is knowing what you own (see "Home Inventory" pages 68-71), and what it would cost to rebuild your home and replace its contents.

Some policies include an inflation clause to keep up with increasing values, but you'd still be wise to know what it would cost to replace everything in your house, and particularly the cost of rebuilding it. From time to time, check with a couple of local builders for the current cost per square foot of building a home.

Replacement policies generally have "caps" or restrictions on coverage. Talk to your agent about what your policy covers specifically—and to what extent.

Riders for Additional Coverage

Most homeowner's policies are written to cover possessions as a percentage of the home's value, with restrictions on amounts and how the loss occurred.

And, there's the issue of proving—or trying to prove—you owned a special item, or several special items, now damaged or stolen.

Jewelry is a good example. If a 1.5-carat diamond engagement ring is stolen, basic coverage would be $1,000. You can't replace the ring for that, but jewelry coverage is limited. If any of the following areas apply to you, talk to your insurance agent about special coverage, or riders, to your basic insurance policy:

- Home office (see right)
- Jewelry
- Oriental rugs
- Art
- Antiques
- If building codes or zoning laws have changed since you bought the house
- If floods or earthquakes are a threat

Saving on Insurance

Sometimes it seems every time you ask about insurance, you end up paying more for coverage. Here are a few ways to save.

☐ If you group your insurance policies—for example, homeowner's, additional liability, car, and/or several riders—you may qualify for a discount of up to 15 percent. And staying with the same company for several years may get you a discount, especially if you've made no or few claims.

☐ Adding a security system to your home can reduce premiums.

☐ Fireproofing your house, adding smoke detectors, or owning a newer home can also make you eligible for policy discounts.

☐ If you're a member of a select group—say a graduate of a certain university or are a senior citizen—special, discounted policies may be offered to you. If taking advantage of the discounts means buying a new policy, be sure to scour it for differences; you may not be getting comparable coverage, so the discount may not be as great as you thought.

Home Office Insurance

If you're a member of the zero-commute group, you need to protect your business interests as well as your home. Insuring just the physical items that are part of your business—the computer, the fax machine, and such—doesn't completely cover your business. To make sure you have enough coverage, you need to consider some less-than-pleasant possibilities.

☐ Think about how you'd run your business in the event a disaster destroyed both home and office. For example, if a fire destroyed your home and office, where would you work until your home is rebuilt? You'd likely need to pay for temporary office space.

☐ A key consideration is protecting your business from the loss of another business's property that is in your possession. If a thief steals your computer or if a virus wipes out the computer's memory and the only copy of your client's sales campaign is on the computer, you may be liable for the loss.

☐ Some possibilities may be covered simply by clarifying and enhancing your homeowner's policy. For example, if a client at your home business takes a fall on the ice outside your door, your regular policy may cover the medical expenses.

☐ If you have any employees, even part-time, they can affect your insurance picture.

As home-based businesses become more popular, insurance companies are offering better coverage options. Talk to several insurance agents about their options.

Fire Safety

A fire can be even more devastating to your family than a burglary. Getting an early warning and knowing how to respond can save lives. According to the National Fire Protection Association, more than 1,000 people are killed every year in the U.S. alone, and thousands more are injured in electrical shock and burn accidents—many of them preventable. Of course, adequately protecting your house against these dangers is the best idea.

Develop a Family Fire Plan

Don't waste precious time and possibly risk your life trying to put out a major fire with an extinguisher. Instead, immediately evacuate everyone from the house and call the fire department from a neighbor's home. To make sure every family member knows how to get out quickly and safely,

prepare and rehearse a fire emergency plan. Here's what it should include.

☐ Identify escape routes. Draw up a floor plan of your home and earmark at least two exits from every room. Doors, of course, are primary exits, but if fire or smoke blocks them, consider windows as secondary escape routes. All windows you need to use for exits should be openable. If a window can't be opened, use a shoe or chair to break the glass and clear away jagged edges. You can also throw a blanket over the sill to protect against cuts. Post your escape plan where baby-sitters and guests can see it.

☐ Pay special attention to upper-floor windows. If some have access to porch roofs, find out if it's safe to use them. For other high windows, position noncombustible chain ladders.

☐ Provide for elderly people and small children. Assign someone to help them out.

☐ Agree on a meeting place. Pick a site outside, such as a tree in the front yard, where you all will gather after an evacuation. This way you will know if the house is vacant or if anyone is still inside. If someone is missing, don't attempt a rescue yourself; fire fighters are equipped and trained for this job.

☐ Hold fire drills. Make some practice runs at night, so everyone knows exactly what to do and where to rendezvous. If you have a chain ladder, make sure everyone knows how to use it.

☐ Close bedroom doors at night. Most fatal home fires begin in rooms other than the bedroom. Fire produces deadly heated gases and smoke that can kill long before the flames reach a person. If a fire occurs in another part of the house, a closed door will keep out gases, smoke, and heat for some time. And, if a fire should start inside a bedroom, a closed door can retard its spread to other rooms.

☐ If you smell smoke, don't rush into a hallway. Instead, drop to your hands and knees, crawl to the door, and put the back of your hand against the closed door. If the door feels cool, brace it with your shoulder (rapidly expanding gases can push it open), cautiously open it, and move your hand across the opening to determine how hot the air is; if it feels cool and flames or smoke aren't pouring up a stairway, you may be able to use this means of escape. But if the door feels warm, don't open it. Instead, use your secondary escape route.

Fire Inspection Checklist

Use this checklist to do a step-by-step inspection of your house, the same way a fire inspector would. Once you've checked an area, make notes about the needed improvements.

In the Basement

☐ Has the furnace been checked by a professional this year? If the unit is five years old or newer, servicing every other year is considered sufficient, but furnaces that get a lot of use should be checked every year. So should older furnaces—each autumn, before the heating season begins.

☐ How is the wiring in your house? Unless you're remodeling, it's pretty tough to know what's going on behind the wallboard, so check any exposed wiring in the basement or attic to get an idea of its condition, making sure the insulation is not frayed and the conduit is not rusty. If you have doubts about any wiring, consult an electrician.

☐ Are there flammable materials down here? Oily rags, stacks of newspapers, empty boxes, and other items you don't really need could spontaneously ignite or feed a blaze that starts some other way. Clearing clutter—especially from the stairway—also makes it easier to escape, should fire break out.

☐ Can you smell gas? Even a faint odor of natural or propane gas is reason enough to shut it off, open the windows, evacuate the house, and call the utility company, your propane supplier, or fire department.

In Main Living Areas

☐ Are all electrical receptacles the three-prong, grounded type? The old two-slot versions should be replaced. If you know the principles of electricity and grounding, you can probably do this job yourself, as shown on page 55. If not, hire an electrician.

☐ Do you have at least one fire extinguisher for each level of your home? Purchase ABC types and locate them near exits. (More about fire extinguishers is on page 52.)

☐ Do you have important phone numbers posted near the telephone? Include your local fire department, hospital emergency room, ambulance service, poison control center, and family physician.

☐ Do you check smoke detectors frequently? Test the batteries every month and replace them annually. To learn about installing and maintaining smoke detectors, see pages 50-51.

On the Deck

☐ Is the grill safely situated? Some localities prohibit using a charcoal grill on a wood deck because sparks could ignite it. The best spot for one is on top of masonry or gravel. Gas grills pose less of a hazard, but locate one well away from railings, benches, and the house.

☐ Is there debris under your deck? The underside of a deck is no place for firewood, dead branches, or yard clippings. Besides having a potential as kindling, they also impede air flow, and if a deck can't "breathe," rot could set in. You're also inviting bugs to take up residence near the house.

In All Bedrooms

☐ Is every bedroom hallway protected by a smoke alarm? Your sense of smell dulls when you sleep; alarms give a life-saving wakeup call.

☐ Are you using portable heating equipment? Wood-burning, kerosene, and electric heaters—in bedrooms or anywhere else—can ignite draperies, clothing, and other flammable items. When you purchase a heater, make sure it's been tested by a reputable organization such as Underwriters Laboratories (UL) or the American Gas Association (AGA). Shut off a heater before you leave the room or go to bed.

In the Attic

☐ Is the wiring in good condition? An unfinished attic offers another opportunity to assess your home's wiring. Again, if you find deteriorated insulation or rusty conduit, consult an electrician.

☐ Do you smell smoke? If you smell smoke when there's a fire in the fireplace, don't use the fireplace until a chimney specialist has checked the flue. A smoky aroma in the attic probably means the chimney needs to be relined.

☐ Has the chimney been cleaned recently? Chimney fires, usually resulting from creosote buildup, claim hundreds of homes every year. Flues for wood-burning stoves should be cleaned annually, fireplace flues every other year.

Childproofing
Your Home

From the moment a baby begins to crawl, home becomes a learning experience, with hundreds of things to look at, touch, and taste. Before your child or grandchild becomes mobile, lock, secure, relocate, or remove anything that may pose a potential danger. Here's a room-by-room checklist that can help protect your little one.

In the Kitchen

☐ Remove cleaning supplies and fluids from lower storage areas or keep them under lock and key, and place the key where your child can't reach it.

☐ Keep electrical and telephone cords bundled and tucked out of reach. Unplug portable appliances when they're not in use.

☐ When cooking, turn pot handles to the back of the stove; use extra care when the oven is on.

☐ If your range has knobs at the front where a toddler could reach them, remove the knobs when the range isn't being used.

☐ Don't use tablecloths; kids can pull them, dropping the table's contents on them and the floor.

☐ Keep sharp knives and other cutting tools in a locked drawer or cabinet.

☐ Many child care experts recommend clearing out a lower kitchen cabinet and stocking it with toys, plastic storage containers, or other safe items to play with when he or she wants to be with Mom or Dad in the kitchen. Also, having a cabinet of his or her own may reduce the temptation to explore other cabinets in the kitchen.

In the Bathroom

☐ Keep everything a child could accidentally ingest—medications, mouthwashes, after-shave lotions, insect repellents, cosmetics, cleaning agents, and drain cleaner—in a key-locked cabinet. Don't depend on "child-resistant" latches; some kids find them easy pickings.

☐ Install toilet lid locks; just a few inches of water poses a danger.

☐ Turn down your water heater to 120 degrees to prevent scalding.

☐ Never leave a small child alone in the bathtub for even "just a second."

☐ Install night lights in bathrooms, bedrooms, and hallways.

In Other Indoor Areas

☐ Cover all unused electrical outlets. Most receptacles are within easy reach of a crawling baby.

☐ Route cords for lamps and other electrical items behind furniture where toddlers can't reach them.

☐ Install gates at stairways, top and bottom.

☐ Lift blind and drapery cords out of the reach of little hands.

☐ Use specially designed door stops and knobs that prevent children from opening forbidden doors.

☐ Many houseplants are toxic. Check with your area's poison control center to find out which ones are, and remove them.

☐ Make the garage off limits. But just in case, be sure any potentially dangerous items are stored out of reach and/or locked up.

☐ Keep garage door opener out of reach.

In the Yard

☐ Remove plants that are poisonous (again, check with your local poison control center) and plants that attract bees.

☐ Keep children away when mowing the grass; a mower can hurl rocks.

☐ Always put away fertilizers, gardening tools, pesticides, lawn mowers, and other potentially harmful tools and supplies.

☐ Make sure fencing is free of sharp or jagged edges, splinters, protruding nails, and peeling paint.

☐ Remove peeling paint from outbuildings and/or your home's exterior. (For information about dealing with lead-based paint, see page 78.)

In a Play Area

A well-planned play area diverts kids' attentions from potential dangers, such as a busy street, and provides a place where they can exercise their bodies and imaginations. In planning play equipment, keep the following points in mind:

☐ Angles or openings must be large enough or small enough so that they can't accidentally entrap a child's head or body.

☐ Eliminate sharp edges, corners, or protrusions.

☐ All screws and bolts should be securely capped.

☐ Hang swings from closed O-rings, not open S-hooks (or pinch S-hooks shut).

☐ Swing ropes must be strong enough to support an adult's weight.

☐ Swing seats should be made from a light, soft material—such as rubber or canvas—that won't cause an injury if the seat hits a child.

☐ Check equipment every so often for loose hardware, posts, and other framework.

☐ A layer of wood chips, pea gravel, or sand cushions falls.

In and Around a Pool

As much as kids love pools, you'd be wise to make sure they have access to your pool only when you're there to supervise. Observe these basic rules:

☐ Don't let children enter a pool area without an adult who can swim.

☐ Don't allow running, pushing, or rough play.

☐ Keep glass and electrical appliances away from the pool area.

☐ Lock up chemicals and equipment.

☐ Have a floating life ring attached to a rope and a rescue crook for pulling a person to the pool's side.

☐ Check local ordinances for the type and height of fencing around your pool. Gates should be self-latching, with locks that are out of a child's reach.

☐ Locate a first-aid kit near the pool.

☐ Install a pool alarm to alert you if someone falls in.

☐ A phone by the pool allows you to answer calls without leaving children unattended—and to summon help more quickly if need be.

☐ Make sure all family members have taken swimming lessons. Knowing how to swim is the best defense against drowning.

Household
Contaminants

Unfortunately, many hazardous substances blend in around us. They emit no foul odors and, unlike in the movies, don't glow bright green. Here are some of the most common contaminants found in houses:

☐ Asbestos was once used extensively in siding, floor tiles, joint compound, and pipe insulation. It's dangerous only if disturbed, and then it releases tiny particles into the air. These abrasive particles are easily breathed in and damage lung tissue. Do not cut, sand, or handle materials that might contain asbestos. If you need to remove an asbestos product, hire an abatement contractor.

☐ Lead was used in paint, water pipes, and pipe solder. Lead-based paint becomes hazardous when it chips off or turns to dust and gets inhaled or swallowed. Exposed paint predating 1978 should be painted over, and lead pipes should be replaced. Soldered copper joints present little danger, but new plumbing should be installed with a lead-free solder.

☐ Formaldehyde is a gas emitted by many building and furnishing components—particleboard and foam, for example. Some people are sensitive to the gas and experience coughing, headaches, dizziness, and nausea. Formaldehyde content is now enforced by federal standards. Fortunately, emissions decrease over time. If you suffer from these symptoms, call your state health department for an air test.

☐ Radon is a radioactive gas generated in the bedrock of some regions of the United States. Radon enters a home through cracks in the home's foundation, and long-term exposure to radon can cause lung cancer. Contact your state health department for testing and abatement information.

☐ Carbon monoxide (CO_2) is an odorless and deadly gas produced by combustion sources, such as furnaces and water heaters, fireplaces, and automobiles. Brief exposure to the gas can cause a sore throat, headache, or drowsiness; long-term exposure can be fatal. The best way to safeguard against CO_2 is to install carbon monoxide detectors near combustion appliances, fireplaces, and the door to an attached garage. Some sound an alarm when the gas is present; others change color. You can also find CO_2 test kits at hardware stores and home centers.

Disposing of Hazardous Waste

Waste management guidelines vary considerably from community to community. Before you dispose of anything that you think might be hazardous, check with a local source, such as your waste collector or waste management agency, your local or state environmental protection department, or the County Extension Service.

Brush cleaners, degreasers, oil-based paint, wood preservatives, and most pesticides present special disposal problems and should not be discarded with everyday household trash. Many communities now sponsor annual or semiannual hazardous waste pickup days for these items or have special hazardous waste drop-off facilities for disposing of these toxic items.

Working With Pressure-Treated Lumber

Pressure-treated (PT) lumber has been saturated with chromated copper arsenic (CCA), which makes it rot-resistant, but also irritating to human tissues. The Environmental Protection Agency has issued these precautions for the handling and use of PT wood products:

☐ *Wear gloves. Wash your hands thoroughly after working with PT wood.*

☐ *Wear a dust mask and protective goggles when you saw or sand the wood. The treatment chemical irritates lungs and eyes.*

☐ *Dispose of scraps by burying them or treating them as ordinary trash. Never burn pressure-treated lumber.*

☐ *Avoid using PT wood where it might come into contact with food or animal feed.*

☐ *Don't use pressure-treated wood for countertops or cutting boards.*

Universal
Design

Universal design is based on the theory that homes and products designed to meet the needs of the least-able user are easier and safer for everyone to

use. Doorways and hallways, for example, are wider than the norm to facilitate easy maneuvering of a wheelchair or walker. Lever-style door handles and faucets replace the round knobs that can be difficult to operate with arthritic hands.

Grab bars make it easier to get in and out of a bathtub or around a toilet.

Universal design, in other words, is thoughtful to whomever lives in a particular house—young, old, tall, short, able-bodied, and disabled—making life easier throughout all life stages.

A Barrier-Free Bath

Ideally, a bath accessible to a wheelchair-user should have a clear area at least 5 feet in diameter. This enables the user to rotate the chair and move freely to each of the fixtures. Also, a clear area 4 feet wide in front of each fixture accommodates the full length of the chair.

Heights are important, too. The toilet seat should be between 19 and 20 inches off the floor (standard seats are 15 to 16 inches). Locate grab bars 33 inches above the floor for support when transferring from the wheelchair to the toilet or into or out of the tub or shower.

The lavatory should be no higher than 34 inches off the floor and should extend 27 inches from the wall. Route water supply and drain lines to free knee space beneath the lavatory, and insulate the hot water supply pipe and drainpipe to prevent burning a wheelchair-user's knees.

A Barrier-Free Kitchen

A kitchen designed with Universal Design principles is a wheelchair cook's dream. It eliminates everyday obstacles and modifies existing spaces to suit a disabled person's needs.

The modifications start with the height of the countertops—30 inches instead of the standard 36 inches. The wall oven is mounted lower, too, at a height convenient for a wheelchair user. The range is a simple cooktop, with controls mounted at the front and the heating elements are staggered so the cook never has to reach across a front unit to put a pot on one at the rear.

Spaces under the cooktop, sink, and other counters enable a wheelchair-user to push his or her

knees under the tops. Storage also is within easy reach. Standard cabinets with pull-out racks put pots and pans within reach. And a lazy Susan in each corner cabinet puts spices, small appliances, and cooking ingredients close at hand.

For More Information

To learn specifics about universal design, contact the Center for Universal Design at 800/647-6777; http://www.design.ncsu.edu/cud

Index

Numbers in **bold** indicate pages with photographs.